PREFACE

On July 20, 2019 United States Attorney General William Barr announced, via the publication of a document titled "The First Step Act Of 2018: Risk And Needs Assessment System", that the final approved, catalogued, and vetted list of recidivism reduction programs and productive activities that could be used by inmates to earn time credits under the First Step Act Of 2018, would NOT be released until January, 2020. Until that time, there is no finally approved specific listing available anywhere. As such, until AG Barr releases approved "list", it is possible, regardless of how unlikely, that the evidence based recidivism reduction programs identified in this book will not be approved by the Attorney General for use in recidivism reduction programming. Having said that, the programs listed in this book have been widely used in the United States and have national recognition as being evidence based; meaning that there is empirical evidence to support the proposition that they reduce recidivism rates in successful program participants. Many thought that Attorney General Barr would have approved *lists* on July 20, 2019, however, that did not happen. Attorney General Barr specifically noted that the approved list will be published in January, 2020, along with an approved listing of "productive activities" that may be pursued by inmates seeking to earn early release time credits. Although the First Step Act Of 2018 did not specifically name <u>any</u> evidence based recidivism programs, per se, the Author has no reason to believe that the six programs cited in this book will not be adopted for use by the Bureau Of Prisons once the final list is published. Conversely, the First Step Act Of 2018 did specifically name a whole host of productive activities that Attorney General Barr should adopt as endorsed productive activities, when the endorsed productive activities list is published in January, 2020.

For further information regarding Attorney General Barr's July 20, 2019 published 102 page document "The First Step Act Of 2018: Risk And Needs Assessment System" see this link: https://www.nij.gov/documents/the-first-step-act-of-2018-risk-and-needs-assessment-system.pdf. Attorney General Barr's July 20, 2019 release does not deal with earned time credits per se, under either recidivism reduction programming or productive activities, but rather, deals with *planned* risk and needs assessment and inmate classification into 4 categories of recidivism risk, First Step Act Of 2018 Bureau Of Prisons implementation, and a synopsis of Department Of Justice activities to date, in compliance with mandates imposed by Congress, including deadline dates for various stages of implementation. This is a massive undertaking and Attorney General Barr has done a fantastic job with implementation to date.

Federal Sentencing Alliance has published a related book titled: "Deconstructing The First Step Act of 2018 Risk and Needs Assessment System, For Inmates Seeking To Maximize Prison Time Credits" that excerpts and analyzes specific provisions within the new risk and needs assessment system known as PATTERN, announced July 20, 2019.

INTRODUCTION

Federal Sentencing Alliance is pleased to provide you with a reformatted and easy to ready text of The First Step Act Of 2018, together with an analysis of certain programs and activities that an inmate may engage in to earn prison time credits for earlier release once these programs are approved, catalogued and vetted for implementation at any particular facility. Time credits are earned from participation and successful completion of recidivism reduction programs and/or many other productive activities, while incarcerated in the federal Bureau Of Prisons. The First Step Act Of 2018 does not apply to State prison sentences. Full implementation of these programs will be ongoing through 2022.

The primary focus of this publication relates to "how to" identify recidivism reduction programs; and "how to" earn recidivism reduction program time credits and/or productive activity time credits, for inmates that otherwise qualify to participate in these programs. Inmates serving sentences imposed as a result of being convicted of offenses ineligible for earned time credits is found at 18 U. S. Code § 3632 (d)(D)(2019). Inmates convicted of those enumerated offenses do not qualify for participation in the early release time credit programs that are the subjects of this book. Inmates are encouraged to look at the disqualification list to ensure their own qualification for these programs, and to be prepared to argue why they are qualified, as needed.

The types of programs an inmate can participate in for earned time credits is dependent upon the results of an initial recidivism risk and needs assessment to be completed by the Bureau Of Prisons no later than January, 2020, under a new system known as the "Prisoner Assessment Tool Targeting Estimated Risk and Needs" or simply "PATTERN". For those inmates that achieve a low or minimal recidivism risk assessment, engaging in *productive activities* will result in earned time credits. The Act even provides for certain inmates to be considered to "deliver" productive activity programs to other inmates. For those that are assessed moderate or higher risk of recidivism, time credits can be earned through participation in *recidivism reduction programs* offered at the facility. It is likely that various programs will be initially available at various Bureau Of Prison facilities at different times during the implementation process.

This book details six separate evidence based recidivism reductions programs widely in use in United States Prison Systems at the time of this publication. Many of these programs have been listed on the National Institute Of Justice website for years, as being evidence based recidivism reduction programs with international recognition. Again, these six programs have not yet been approved by Attorney General Barr who has stated that the approved "list" will be released in January, 2020. There is much incentive for a federal inmate to engage in approved recidivism reduction programming to greatly reduce actual time spent in prison. The First Step Act Of 2018 is geared toward rewarding certain model inmates, and others who are striving to become model inmates, via application of earned time credits applied retroactively on the last day of their respective sentences. Until the last day, the Bureau Of Prisons has authority to revoke time credits otherwise earned, for bad behavior.

The purpose of this book is to wade through and clarify the earned time credit provisions of the First Step Act Of 2018, and to foster an inmate's use of those provisions to better his or her own life in the process. These programs are all geared toward 'learning', which by definition aid in personal and professional growth, make available time easier to bear, and give one hope for the future. These programs will invariably give thousands of federal inmate's a new found purpose while incarcerated, and provide them with a vast array of educational tools that were not utilized by them prior to their own incarceration.

Federal Sentencing Alliance is not associated with the United States Congress, the Bureau Of Prisons, or any agency or department of the United States. The First Step Act Of 2018, it's implementation, and final parameters, is within the sound province of the Attorney General Of The United States, the Bureau Of Prisons, and other federal departments and agencies.

Any opinions expressed by Federal Sentencing Alliance should not be construed as legal advice. The analysis and opinions expressed by Federal Sentencing Alliance in this book regarding earned time credits for early release, based upon successful participation and completion of recidivism reduction programs and/or productive activities, represent the opinions of Federal Sentencing Alliance alone, intended to foster critical thinking regarding these topics. Because program implementation will be ongoing until 2022 there will be plenty of critical thinking in the process at various stages of implementation to finality.

Federal Sentencing Alliance ("FSA") headquartered in Florida, is a national consortium of federal sentencing mitigation specialists, federal sentencing legal writers, and supervisory members, that works directly with individual attorneys and law firms based in the United States for all federal sentencing assignments. FSA has various Service Plans to suit your needs.

FSA specializes in federal plea agreement assessment (pre or post signing), extensive federal sentencing mitigation investigation and documentation, probation department liaison, and all related federal sentencing document drafting, conformed for your final edit, including: the pre-PSR Mitigation Package, the Response To Pre-Sentence Report, the Federal Sentencing Memorandum, and all Appendices for these filings, together with all caselaw and documentary references cited.

FSA offers additional services related to Commission datafiles (raw data) analysis on a case by case basis; and other services tied to interactions with the Bureau Of Prisons regarding timely implementation of The First Step Act Of 2018 earned recidivism reduction program and productive activity time credits.

FSA offers complete federal pre sentencing mitigation investigation services simultaneously with federal sentencing document drafting services for all federal criminal cases nationwide at all stages of the prosecution; for attorneys and law firms only.

Please visit our Website for a full list of services found at: www.FederalSentencingAlliance.com.

Please visit out Information Website for the Word version of the Federal Sentencing Guidelines, updated annually, found at: www.FederalSentencingGuidelines.us.

TABLE OF CONTENTS

First Step Act Time Credit Provisions   1

What Does It Mean?   1

Operative Implementation Questions   2

Mandatory Timing Of First Step Act Implementation Dates   4

The Bureau Of Prisons Deadline Dates   4

Full Implementation Dates Summary   5

Legal Rights Without Solid Remedies?   5

A Call For Pro-Activity For A Federal Inmate's Time Credits   6

Proactive Inmates   6

Six Evidence Based Recidivism Reduction Programs   9

The Big 6 Recidivism Reduction Programs List   11

Program 1: Aggression Replacement Training (ART)   11

Program 2: Strategies For Self Improvement & Change (SSC)   13

Program 3: Moral Reconation Therapy (MRT)   17

Program 4: Reasoning & Rehabilitation (R&R)   21

Program 5: Relapse Prevention Therapy (RPT)   24

Program 6: Thinking For A Change (T4C)   26

Engaging In Productive Activities For Earned Time Credits   29

Correspondence College Courses Through The Mail As Productive Activities   30

The First Step Act of 2018 (Reformatted Easy to Read Text)   32 - 128

First Step Act Of 2018 - Bureau Of Prisons Recidivism Reduction Programs & Productive Activities Time Credits

One of the major provisions of the First Step Act Of 2018 enables inmates convicted of certain non-violent and non-heinous offenses to earn prison program and activity "time credits" applied to successfully earned earlier release.

First Step Act Of 2018 Time Credits Provision:

The "time credit" provisions of the Act have been codified into 18 U.S. Code § 3632 (2019), that now reads:

"(4) Time credits.-

(A) In general. A prisoner, except for an ineligible prisoner under subparagraph (D), who successfully completes evidence based recidivism reduction programming or productive activities, shall earn time credits as follows:

(i) A prisoner shall earn 10 days of time credits for every 30 days of successful participation in evidence-based recidivism reduction programming or productive activities.

(ii) A prisoner determined by the Bureau of Prisons to be at a minimum or low risk for recidivating, who, over 2 consecutive assessments, has not increased their risk of recidivism, shall earn an additional 5 days of time credits for every 30 days of successful participation in evidence-based recidivism reduction programming or productive activities." *Id.*

What does that mean?

1. A prisoner with a non-violent qualifying offense(s), who receives a recidivism risk assessment and is deemed to have a low or minimal risk of recidivism, can sign up for "productive activities" and get a 10 day time credit for every 30 days successfully spent engaged in productive activities while incarcerated. That same prisoner after receiving a second

consecutive low or minimum risk of recidivism assessment, can up their time credits from 10 to 15 days for every 30 days successfully spent engage in productive activities.

2. A prisoner with non-violent qualifying offense(s), who receives a recidivism risk assessment and is deemed to have a moderate or higher risk of recidivism, can sign up for "evidence based recidivism reduction programming" and still get the same 10 day time credit for every 30 days successfully spent engaged in recidivism reduction programs, while incarcerated. That same prisoner would also have incentive with hard work toward achieving two consecutive low or minimum recidivism risk assessments, in order to be aptly rewarded by earning an additional 5 days of time credits per 30 days spent successfully engaged in those continued programs; and to open the door for the same 15/30 time credits available spent successfully engaged in productive activities.

Operative Implementation Questions:

These are some pressing questions for those who could be taking advantage of time credit programs now, but are waiting for time credit programs to become fully operational:

1. How long will it take to get a recidivism risk assessment?

2. How long will it take the BOP to implement sufficient recidivism reduction programs for everybody that needs them?

3. Are there provisions for continuous recidivism reduction programs and/or productive activities at all facilities?

4. How long will it take to get the maximum time credits available under the law?

Although not written, it appears that many inmates who could benefit from prison time credits under the Act, either will not benefit from them, or will not benefit fully, due to the

2

inherent time lags at the Bureau Of Prisons implementing and expanding the programs necessary to comply with the Act's mandates, and considering an inmates otherwise scheduled release date.

The First Step Act Of 2018 was signed on December 21, 2018 by President Trump and became law on that date. There will be many inmates desirous to cap their earned time credits in the short term and going forward that may become frustrated, because the system is not fully in place or fully operational at their facility, when they want it to be. The Congress recognized that the new system requires time to implement, cross check and balances, auditing, empirical studies and research, trial and error, and further reporting to Congress.

The Bureau Of Prisons was given authority to immediately react to the Act's provisions for preparing the infrastructure and programming necessary to implement the Act's program time credits; 18 U.S. Code § 3621 (h)(4) was amended to include immediate authority:

> "(4) Preliminary expansion of evidence-based recidivism reduction programs and authority to use incentives.—
>
> Beginning on the date of enactment of this subsection, the Bureau of Prisons may begin to expand any evidence-based recidivism reduction programs and productive activities that exist at a prison as of such date, and may offer to prisoners who successfully participate in such programs and activities the incentives and rewards described in subchapter D." *Id.*
>
> [Use of the term "may" means that it was not mandatory that the BOP "begin" to expand it's programs as of December 21, 2018.]
>
> Indeed, it is not "mandatory" for the Bureau Of Prisons to "begin" to expand any

evidence based recidivism reduction programs and productive activities, until January 15, 2020, pursuant to 18 U.S. Code § 3621(h)(1), infra.

Mandatory Timing Of First Step Act Implementation Dates:

The Attorney General's Office First Deadline Date:

1.) 18 U.S. Code § 3632(a) says that the Attorney General has 210 days from December 21, 2018 to publish a Website titled: "risk and needs assessment system"; that being on or before, July 19, 2019. This is intended to be a non-clinical assessment checklist type form that is completed commensurate with an inmate's initial intake into a facility, replacing the 2006 risk assessment system in place prior to the First Step Act Of 2018, that did not consider an inmate's "needs" or "recidivism reduction" per se.

The Bureau Of Prisons Deadline Dates:

1.) As stated above, 18 U.S. Code § 3621(h)(1) gives the Bureau Of Prisons through January 15, 2020, 180 days from July 19, 2019, to implement and complete the initial intake of risk and needs assessment for each prisoner; and to begin to "expand" and to "add" any new "evidence based recidivism reduction" and "productive activities" programs "necessary to effectively implement the system".

2.) Next, 18 U.S. Code § 3621(h)(2) gives the Bureau Of Prisons through January 15, 2022 to make sure that all prisoners get the maximum benefit of recidivism reduction and productive activities programming time credits; and to have inmates reassessed for recidivism as necessary to achieve the maximum credits available.

Full Implementation Dates Summary:

In sum, the First Step Act Of 2018 gives the Bureau Of Prisons through January 15, 2022, to make recidivism reduction and productive activities programming fully operational for the maximum achievable benefit for all inmates endeavoring to enter into these programs full time to earn time credits for early release.

Legal Rights Without Solid Remedies?

Although the First Step Act Of 2018 confers early release rights to inmates, including the rights to participate in and earn recidivism reduction and productive activities program time credits, those rights are officially deferred, subject to the fully operational program deadline date of January 15, 2022. Additionally, the Congress made all program time credits and their application to any particular inmate, within the sound province of the Bureau Of Prisons, which appears to have the ultimate authority over these matters. The First Step Act Of 2018 does not give an inmate standing per se to complain to any court for relief regarding any perceived misapplication of prison time credits to any sentence, or for any other prison program time credit complaint.

Regardless of whether the Act confers standing to an inmate to complain or not, at least one Bureau Of Prisons inmate did just that resulting in the inmate's early release under the Act in 2019 anyway. *See United States Of America vs. Hassan Nemazee*, United States District Court Southern District Of New York, Case No.: 1:09-cr-902-SHS. The Nemazee court made no ruling whether Nemazee had standing to file for early release, pursuant to the First Step Act Of 2018, or not. The issue was never reached, because the Bureau Of Prisons just agreed to release Nemazee while his Motion was pending. *See Id.* [DE 133][DE 149] It is likely that the Bureau Of Prisons will be inundated with requests from inmates to retroactively apply time credits for early release, pursuant to the First Step Act Of 2018. The Nemazee case did not pertain to recidivism reduction or productive activities time credits, which cannot be retroactively applied, but rather dealt with other retroactive time credits applied to Nemazee's sentence. The point being, Nemazee found a way to get the Court to entertain his motion regardless of whether the Court had jurisdiction to hear his Motion or not.

A Call For Proactivity For A Federal Inmate's Time Credits:

Although the Bureau Of Prisons is likely working on First Step Act Of 2018 time credit programming for recidivism reduction and productive activities implementation now, the Act gives the Bureau until January 15, 2022 to become fully up and running due to an extended phase in process. In the meantime, many current and prospective inmate's may not get either the benefit or full benefit of these planned programs due to timing issues. As previously stated, 18 U.S. Code § 3621(h)(4) gave the Bureau Of Prisons authority to start working on phase in processes as of December 21, 2018. In that regard, the Bureau Of Prisons started working on getting recidivism reduction programs lined up, and more certified instructors trained, even before the First Step Act Of 2018 became law, in anticipation that this non partisan bill would pass the House and Senate and would become law. Kudos to the Bureau Of Prisons for it's insight in that regard.

Proactive Inmates:

The pinnacle question now is whether the Bureau Of Prisons will permit individual inmates to become part of these ground breaking processes at their facilities or not; and whether the Bureau Of Prisons has considered utilizing current inmates as part of these

implementation processes themselves. The pinnacle answer is that they should. This is why:

18 U.S. Code § 3635(5)(2019) grants the Bureau Of Prisons authority to utilize local inmate

talent to "deliver" the programs earmarked for earned time credits, within the sole discretion

of the Bureau Of Prisons. *See* 18 U.S. Code § 3635(3)(2019), *infra*.

> 18 U.S. Code § 3635(5)(2019) states:
>
> "Productive activity.-The term "productive activity" means either a group or individual activity that is designed to allow prisoners determined as having a minimum or low risk of recidivating to remain productive and thereby maintain a minimum or low risk of recidivating, and *may include the delivery of the programs described in paragraph (1)*[1] *to other prisoners.*" Id.
>
> 18 U.S. Code § 3635(3)(2019) states:
>
> "(3) EVIDENCE-BASED RECIDIVISM REDUCTION PROGRAM.-The term "evidence-based recidivism reduction program" means either a group or individual activity that-
>
>> (A) has been shown by empirical evidence to reduce recidivism or is based on research indicating that it is likely to be effective in reducing recidivism;
>>
>> (B) is designed to help prisoners succeed in their communities upon release from prison; and
>>
>> (C) may include-
>>
>>> (i) social learning and communication, interpersonal, anti-bullying, rejection response, and other life skills;

---

[1]   The United States House Of Representatives noted a typographical error in the text of the First Step Act Of 2018, noting "should be paragraph (3)", not "paragraph (1)". See http://law2.house.gov/view.xhtml?req=granuleid:USC-prelim-title18-section3635&num=0&edition=prelim dated July 5, 2019. See also 18 U.S. Code § 3635(5)(2019).

(ii) family relationship building, structured parent-child interaction, and parenting skills;

(iii) classes on morals or ethics;

(iv) academic classes;

(v) cognitive behavioral treatment;

(vi) mentoring;

(vii) substance abuse treatment;

(viii) vocational training;

(ix) faith-based classes or services;

(x) civic engagement and re integrative community services;

(xi) a prison job, including through a prison work program;

(xii) victim impact classes or other restorative justice programs; and

(xiii) trauma counseling and trauma-informed support programs." *Id.*

At first blush, it seems that some inmates may be able to present a program to the Warden of the facility where they happen to be incarcerated, and thereafter, become part of that facility's programming to teach classes that fall within evidence based recidivism reduction programming and/or productive activities at the facility. What better way to ensure receipt of maximum time credits under the First Step Act Of 2018 than to be an inmate who actually teaches a class or leads a productive activities group, as a group leader!

Outside Agencies And Third Party Vendors Open Door Policy?

The Act does provide for the Bureau Of Prisons to interact with third parties for the establishment and implementation of recidivism reduction and productive activity programming, which opens the door to communication with individual facilities on these topics; and perhaps, even as these issues pertain to any particular inmate. These issues are all ground breaking and likely will be for quite some time. There will be a learning curve and education regarding the major tenets of the First Step Act Of 2018 and program time credits is ongoing now.

Although the First Step Act Of 2018 provides the shovel to break ground on these issues, any individual facility will still need to establish a network of people in the locale to implement the necessary programming and make it successful on a continuum; all before January 15, 2022. There are no legal reasons why inmates with a low or minimum risk of recidivism themselves cannot be utilized in this process to deliver programs to other inmates in exchange for time credits earned for early release. That should be food for thought for becoming pro active in the Bureau Of Prisons programming implementation processes to the extent it is welcomed by any given facility.

Evidence Based Recidivism Reduction Programs:

SIX EVIDENCE BASED RECIDIVISM RISK PROGRAMS

Endorsed Cognitive-Behavioral Therapy ("CBT") Programs For Offenders

CBT programs are empirically based recidivism reduction programs largely taught in the United State prison systems, where available. The First Step Act of 2018 mandates that the Bureau Of Prisons implement recidivism reduction programs that have been shown by empirical evidence to reduce recidivism. Here are a six recidivism reduction programs that have been shown by empirical studies and research to reduce risk of recidivism when properly administered.

CBT programs, in general, are directed toward changing distorted or dysfunctional cognitions or teaching new cognitive skills and involve structured learning experiences designed to affect such cognitive processes. These processes include interpreting social cues, identifying and compensating for distortions and errors in thinking, generating alternative solutions, and making decisions about appropriate behavior.

Traditional cognitive-behavioral approaches used with correctional populations have been designed as either cognitive-restructuring, coping-skills, or problem solving therapies. The cognitive restructuring approach views problem behaviors as a consequence of maladaptive or dysfunctional thought processes, including cognitive distortions, social misperceptions, and faulty logic (e.g., Ross and Fabiano, 1985). The coping-skills approaches focus on improving deficits in an offender's ability to adapt to stressful situations. Problem-solving therapies focus on offenders' behaviors and skills (rather than their thought processes) as the element that is ineffective and maladaptive (Mahoney and Arnkoff, 1978). One study observed that most cognitive-behavioral programs developed for criminal offenders tend to be of the first type, focusing on cognitive deficits and distortions (Henning and Frueh, 1996).

Effective cognitive-behavioral programs of all types attempt to assist offenders in four primary tasks: (1) define the problems that led them into conflict with authorities, (2) select goals, (3) generate new alternative prosocial solutions, and (4) implement these solutions (Cullen and Gendreau, 2000).

Generally, cognitive-behavioral therapies in correctional settings consist of highly structured treatments that are detailed in manuals (Dobson and Khatri, 2000) and typically delivered to groups of 8 to 12 individuals in a classroom like setting. Highly individualized, one-on-one cognitive-behavioral therapy provided by mental health professionals is not practical on a large scale within the prison system (Wilson, Bouffard, and Mackenzie, 2005).

There are six cognitive-behavioral programs that are widely used in the prison system and criminal justice system[2]. Here is the Big 6 list that will be examined in turn:

---

[2] These six (6) have been endorsed by the United States Department Of Justice-Office Of Justice Programs, National Instituted Of Justice ("NIJ"), for years, and there is no reason to believe that these will not be fully incorporated into implementation of The First Step Act Of 2018. The information provided here regarding these six evidence based recidivism reduction programs was originally published by NIJ on it's website. Attorney General Barr has already examined these programs, but has yet to finally include them in the final list of approved,

The Big 6 Recidivism Reduction Programs:

#1   Aggression Replacement Training® (ART®) (Goldstein and Glick, 1987).

#2   Criminal Conduct and Substance Abuse Treatment: Strategies for Self Improvement and Change (SSC) (Wanberg and Milkman, 1998, 2007 in press).

#3   Moral Reconation Therapy® (MRT®) (Little and Robinson, 1986).

#4   Reasoning and Rehabilitation (R&R and R&R2) (Ross and Fabiano,1985).

#5   Relapse Prevention Therapy (RPT) (Parks and Marlatt, 1999).

#6   Thinking for a Change (T4C) (Bush, Glick, and Taymans, 1997).

To date, MRT and R&R, have been more prevalently examined with respect to outcome evaluation (Wilson, Bouffard, and Mackenzie, 2005).

A description of each of the primary CBT programs for offenders is provided below along with summaries of published studies of program evaluation (when available) .

Program #1:   Aggression Replacement Training® (ART):

[ART is an adolescent program, not a recidivism risk reduction program delivered to adults. ART description is included here for completeness purposes.]

Aggression Replacement Training® (ART®)[3] is a multimodal intervention originally designed to reduce anger and violence among adolescents involved with juvenile justice systems (Goldstein and Glick, 1987). More recently, the model has been adapted for use in adult correctional settings.

Based on previous work with at-risk youth, ART seeks to provide youngsters with prosocial skills to use in antisocial situations as well as skills to manage anger impulses that lead to aggressive and violent actions. It also seeks to increase their ability to view their world in a more fair and equitable manner by taking others' perspectives into account. Thus, ART is designed to train youngsters in what to do in anger-producing situations, using social skills training (Bandura, 1973; Goldstein et al., 1978); what not to do in anger producing situations, using anger control training (Feindler, Marriott, and Iwata, 1984); and to consider others' perspectives using moral reasoning (Kohlberg, 1969; Gibbs and Potter, 1995). ART takes

---

catalogued, and vetted recidivism risk reduction programs. As of the date of this publication, there is NO approved list in place, however, that will change shortly. The approved list will be published in January, 2020 by the Bureau Of Prisons.

[3] Aggression Replacement Training® (ART®) was awarded trademarks in 2004 by the U.S .Patent and Trademark Office protecting printed matter and training seminars, training programs, and their variants .

methods from each of these models and synthesizes them into a cognitive-behavioral intervention.

Social Skills Training

Social skills training (the behavioral component) teaches interpersonal skills to deal with anger-provoking events. It is based on the assumption that aggressive and violent youth have skill deficits and that this is related to their offending behaviors. The 10 social skills (5 cognitive and 5 affective) are:

■Making a compliment.
■Understanding the feelings of others.
■Getting ready for difficult conversations.
■Dealing with someone else's anger.
■Keeping out of fights.
■Helping others.
■Dealing with accusations.
■Dealing with group pressure.
■Expressing affections.
■Responding to failure.

Anger Control Training

Anger control training (the affective component) seeks to teach at-risk youth skills to reduce their affective impulses to behave with anger by increasing their self-control competencies (Feindler, 1981; Novaco, 1975; Meichenbaum, 1977). Youth learn to identify those factors that create their anger and roleplay ways to competently use self-control techniques. Topics include:

■Triggers (external events that cause emotions and the internal statements that increase angry responses).
■Cues (physical reactions that indicate anger arousal).
■Anger reducers (counting backwards, deep breathing, pleasant imagery).
■Reminders (self-statements that instruct youth in ways to reduce, reinterpret, or diffuse angry emotions and/or aggression).
■Self-evaluation (self-rewarding and self-coaching techniques to improve performance).
■Thinking ahead ("if-then" statements to identify consequences for one's actions).

Once youth have reduced their anger arousal by using these techniques, they decide upon an appropriate social skill (that they have already learned in social skills training) to use in an anger-provoking situation.

Moral Reasoning

Moral reasoning (the cognitive component) is a set of procedures designed to raise the young person's level of fairness, justice, and concern with the needs and rights of others.

Youth attend an hour-long class in each of these components (on separate days) each week for 10 weeks. ART is usually part of a differential program, prescriptively chosen to meet the needs of aggressive/violent youth (Glick, 2006, Goldstein and Stein, 1976).

Facilitator Training

The authors of this program of the ART intervention place a strong emphasis on maintaining the integrity of its original design and have developed an accreditation process for those delivering the program. A detailed list of standards and practices, the criteria used to deliver ART, and specific training information is available from G & G Consultants, LLC at *www.g-gconsultants.org*.

Three levels of training are offered including:

■Group Facilitator (Trainer), a 36- to 40-hour didactic seminar.
■Trainer of Group Facilitator (Trainer), a minimum 4- or 5-day, 32- to 40-hour seminar that may include up to 280 hours of additional study once the group facilitators have implemented the program three times with their clients under supervision.
■Master Trainer, an individualized program for those with at least 5 years' experience delivering the program and at least 3 years as a trainer of group trainers.

Training materials used include *Aggression Replacement Training* (Goldstein, Glick, and Gibbs, 1998) and *Aggression Replacement Training: A Comprehensive Intervention for Aggressive Youth* (Goldstein and Glick, 1987)

Program #2: Criminal Conduct and Substance Abuse Treatment: Strategies for Self-Improvement and Change (SSC)

Strategies for Self-Improvement and Change (SSC) was developed by Kenneth Wanberg and Harvey **Milkman** (authors of this publication). It provides a standardized, structured, and well-defined approach to the treatment of clients who manifest substance abuse and criminal justice problems. It is a long-term (9 months to 1 year), intensive, cognitive-behavioral-oriented treatment program for adult substance-abusing offenders. The recommended client age is 18 years or older. However, some older adolescents may benefit from portions of the curriculum.

SSC can be presented in either a community or an incarceration setting. Phase I, which culminates in a comprehensive relapse and recidivism prevention plan, can serve as a stand-alone program that may be followed by Phases II and III either in aftercare settings or while monitored by correctional supervisory personnel.

SSC is behavioral oriented, skill based, and multimodal. It attends to both extra personal circumstances (events) and intrapersonal processes (thoughts, emotions, beliefs, attitudes) that lead to criminal conduct and substance abuse. The treatment curriculum for SSC consists of 12 treatment modules that are structured around the 3 phases of treatment. Each module is taught in a logical sequence with basic topics covered first, serving as the foundation for more difficult concepts covered later. Sessions are divided into three parts:

■Session introduction and rationale, which includes session objectives and key words.
■Session content and focus, which includes all of the exercises and worksheets.
■Summary of session activities and process group, which includes a scale that clients use to rate their level of knowledge and skills learned in the session and suggested topics for the group.

Overview of the SSC Treatment Program

Phase I: Challenge to Change.

This phase involves the client in a reflective contemplative process. A series of lesson experiences is used to build a working relationship with the client and to help the client develop motivation to change. Sessions are also directed at providing basic information on how people change, the role of thought and behavior in change, and basic information about substance abuse and criminal conduct. A major focus of Phase I is to help the client develop self-awareness through self-disclosure and receiving feedback. The assumption underlying this approach is that self-disclosure leads to self-awareness, which in turn leads to self-improvement and change.

The client is confronted with his or her own past and then challenged to bring that past into a present change focus. The goal is to get the client to define the specific areas of change

14

and to commit to that change. This phase includes a review of the client's current alcohol/other drug use and criminal conduct, with the results of this review becoming a focus of the reflective-contemplative process. Each client undergoes an in depth assessment of his or her life situation and problems and looks carefully at the critical areas that need change and improvement. The individual identifies targets of change and, through ongoing process group feedback and counselor/client collaboration, develops a comprehensive relapse and recidivism prevention plan.

Phase II: Commitment to Change.

This phase involves an active demonstration of implementing and practicing change. The focus is on strengthening basic skills for change and learning key CBT methods for changing thought and behavior that contribute to substance abuse and criminal conduct. Themes of these sessions include coping and social skills training with an emphasis on communication skills; managing and changing negative thoughts and thinking errors; recognizing and managing high-risk situations; managing cravings and urges that lead to alcohol and other drug use and criminal conduct; developing self-control through problem solving and assertiveness training; managing thoughts and feelings related to anger, aggression, guilt and depression; understanding and developing close relationships; and understanding and practicing empathy and prosocial values and moral development. Social responsibility therapy (SRT) is a strong part of Phase II.

Phase III: Ownership of Change.

This phase, the stabilization and maintenance phase, involves the client's demonstration of ownership of change over time. This involves treatment experiences designed to reinforce and strengthen the commitment to established changes. This phase includes a review of the concepts of relapse and recidivism prevention and sessions on critical reasoning, conflict resolution, and establishing and maintaining a healthy lifestyle. Change is strengthened though helping the client become involved in a variety of auxiliary methods, including mentoring, role modeling, self-help groups, and other community-based recovery maintenance resources. This phase also provides skills training in managing work and leisure time activities.

Screening and Assessment

An important component of SSC is the screening and assessment process. The client is engaged in the assessment process as a partner with the provider, with the understanding that assessment information is just as valuable to the client as to the provider and that change is based on self-awareness. One module is devoted to engaging the client in an in-depth, differential assessment process, having the client investigate areas of change that are needed, and then constructing a master profile and a master assessment plan that the client can use as a guide for change. A variety of instruments and procedures are recommended to enhance this partnership assessment approach.

An effective assessment approach recognizes that there is a general influence of certain problems on a person's life and within that problem area there occurs a wide variety of differences among people (Wanberg and Horn, 1987). For example, alcohol has a general influence on the life of the alcohol-dependent individual. Yet, individuals who have alcohol problems differ greatly. Some are social drinkers and others drink at bars; some have physical problems from drinking and others do not; some drink continuously, some periodically.

Assessment, then, should consider these two levels of evaluation. Assessment of the general influence is the basis of screening. Looking at the more specific influences and problem areas involves the application of a differential or multidimensional assessment.

SSC structures the differential assessment around five broad areas:

■**Assessment of alcohol and other drug (AOD) use and abuse.** Inclusion guidelines for AOD services are provided with both minimum symptom criteria and descriptions of psychometric tests. The framework includes identifying the types of drugs used and the perceived benefits and real consequences and concerns of use. The assessment process employs a variety of tools, including self-report questionnaires and participation in reflection groups .

■**Assessment of criminal conduct.** A key focus in this assessment area is the extent of antisocial patterns, including criminal associations and criminal attitudes. Risk factor assessment focuses on the modifiable, crime-inducing needs of the offender. Another area of assessment is the identification of patterns of criminal thinking and thinking errors . The "thought report" is a foundational assessment tool used throughout this process .

■**Assessment of cognitive and affective (emotional) processing.** Through assessment, understanding, conceptualizing, and intervening, treatment helps the client to understand and control emotions and actions, which in turn will influence his or her thought processes.

■**Assessment of life-situation problems.** There are several areas of assessment other than AOD and criminal conduct that SSC addresses at both the screening and more in-depth levels of evaluation. These areas are social-interpersonal adjustment; psychological-emotional adjustment; work and finances; marriage, family, and relationships; and health.

■Assessment of motivation and readiness for treatment. Work on stages of change (Prochaska and DiClemente, 1992; Prochaska, DiClemente, and Norcross, 1992) has made it clear that an essential component of assessment is that of determining the client's readiness and motivation for treatment. The area of treatment motivation and readiness should be assessed during the clinical intake interview. A number of questions and issues can be addressed to evaluate this area: willingness to be involved in treatment; whether the person feels a need for help at the present time; whether the client has thought about making changes in particular areas; whether the client has actually made deliberate changes; the degree of problem awareness; and whether others feel that the client should make changes or needs help.

Facilitator Training

Facilitator training sessions in SSC methods run for a total of 26 hours and are held frequently across the United States. They are presented twice annually through the Center for Interdisciplinary Services in Denver, Colorado.

Program #3:   Moral Reconation Therapy® (MRT)

Developed by Greg Little and Ken Robinson between 1979 and 1983 for use in prison-based drug treatment therapeutic communities, Moral Reconation Therapy® (MRT®)[4] is a trademarked and copyrighted cognitive-behavioral treatment program for offenders, juveniles, substance abusers, and others with "resistant personalities." Although initially designed specifically for criminal justice-based drug treatment, MRT has since been expanded for use with offenders convicted of driving while intoxicated (DWI), domestic violence, and sex offenses; parenting skill and job attitude improvement; and to address general antisocial thinking.

The term "moral reconation" was coined in 1972. "Conation" is an archaic term that was used in psychology until the 1930s, when the term "ego" replaced it. It refers to the conscious, decision making portion of one's personality.

"Reconation" implies a reevaluation of decisions. "Moral" indicates the process of making correct, prosocial decisions about behaviors. MRT is based on the experiences of its authors, who noted that offenders were often highly functional during stays in therapeutic

---

[4] Moral Reconation Therapy® (**MRT®**) was awarded its first federal trademark in 1995.

communities but returned to criminal behaviors after release. They felt that the offenders' character and personality traits that led to failure were not being addressed.

The underlying theory of MRT is that offenders and drug abusers have low moral reasoning. It is based on Lawrence Kohlberg's (1976) theory that moral development progresses through six stages and only a few members of the adult population attain the highest level (see Wilson, Bouffard, and MacKenzie, 2005). MRT's authors state that "clients enter treatment with low levels of moral development, strong narcissism, low ego/identity strength, poor self-concept, low self-esteem, inability to delay gratification, relatively high defensiveness, and relatively strong resistance to change and treatment" (Little and Robinson, 1986, p. 135). These traits lead to criminal activity, whereas those who have attained high levels of moral development are not likely to behave in a way that is harmful to others or violates laws. MRT is designed to improve clients' reasoning levels from self-centered ones to those that involve concern for the welfare of others and for societal rules. It draws a clear connection between thought processes and behavior (Wilson, Bouffard, and MacKenzie, 2005) .

The program was initially used at the Federal Correctional Institute in Memphis and continued to be refined until Little and Robinson's workbook for adult offenders entitled *How to Escape Your Prison* was published in 1986. It has been revised numerous times since. In 1987, MRT was implemented at Memphis's Shelby County Jail for use with female offenders. The program continued to expand, and today MRT is used in more than 40 states as well as Canada and Puerto Rico .

Nine personality stages of anticipated growth and recovery are identified in the program:

■**Disloyalty:** Typified by self-centered behavior and a willingness to be dishonest and blame and victimize others .

■**Opposition:** Includes the same behaviors as "disloyalty," only occurring less often .

■**Uncertainty:** Person is unsure of how he or she stands with or feels about others; these individuals still make decisions based on their own pain or pleasure .

■**Injury:** Destructive behavior still occurs, but recognition of the source of the problem also occurs; some responsibility for behavior is taken and some decisions may be based on consequences for others .

■**Nonexistence:** Person feels alienated from things but has a few satisfying relationships; these individuals sway between making decisions based on formal rules and decisions based on pleasure and pain .

■**Danger:** Person commits to goals and makes decisions primarily on law
and societal values; when regression occurs, these individuals experience
anguish and loss of self-esteem.

■**Emergency:** Social considerations are made, but "idealized ethical principles"
influence decision making.

■**Normal:** These individuals are relatively happy, contented people,
who have chosen the right goals for themselves and are fulfilling them
properly; decision making based on pleasure and pain has been virtually
eliminated.

■**Grace:** The majority of decisions are based on ethical principles;
supposedly, only a small percentage of adults reach this stage.

Curriculum

**MRT is conducted in open-ended groups that may meet once a month or up to five
times per week. Group size can vary from 5 to more than 20.** Groups are structured and
address issues such as:

■Confronting personal beliefs.
■Assessing relationships.
■Facilitating identity development.
■Enhancing self-esteem.
■Decreasing hedonism.
■Developing tolerance for the delay of gratification.
Homework tasks and exercises are completed outside of the group and then
presented to group members during meetings. MRT does not require high
reading skills or high mental functioning levels, as participants' homework
includes making drawings or writing short answers. The most important
aspect of the treatment is when the participant shares work with the group.

Note: The parameters of MRT 'meeting up to five times per week' permits the same
inmate to have much more actual class time than other Programs that suggest no more than 2-
3 meeting per week for 90 minutes, such as the T4C Program, infra. The operative question
then becomes whether the T4C 22 week Program will still give a participating inmate time
credits for that entire period, notwithstanding that only 90 minutes per week are spent in the
classroom. Since all of these programs have homework assignments they should. If that is a
concern going into the study, then MRT should be considered better for that sole reason.

The facilitator is trained to ask appropriate questions concerning the exercises and to maintain focus on the participants' completion of MRT's 16 steps, which are:

■**Steps 1 and 2:** Client must demonstrate honesty and trust.
■**Step 3:** Client must accept rules, procedures, treatment requirements, and other people.
■**Step 4:** Client builds genuine self-awareness.
■**Step 5:** Client creates a written summary to deal with relationships that have been damaged because of substance abuse or other antisocial behavior.
■**Step 6:** Client begins to uncover the right things to do to address the causes of unhappiness.
■**Step 7:** Client sets goals.
■**Step 8:** Client refines goals into a plan of action.
■**Step 9:** Client must continue to meet timetables he or she set up.
■**Step 10:** Client conducts a moral assessment of all elements of his or her life.
■**Step 11:** Client reassesses relationships and forms a plan to heal damage to them.
■**Step 12:** Client sets new goals, for 1 year, 5 years, and 10 years, with a focus on how accomplishment of the goals will relate to happiness.
■**Steps 13-16 (optional):** Involves client's confrontation of the self with a focus on an awareness of self. Goals continue to be defined and expanded to include the welfare of others.

Activities

These activities are mandatory for clients in Moral Reconation Therapy:

■Client must become honest at the beginning of the treatment.
■Client must display trust in the treatment program, other clients, and staff .
■Client must become honest in relationships with others and actively work on improving relationships .
■Client must begin actively to help others in need of help and accept nothing in return; he or she must perform a major amount of public service work for those in need (again, accepting nothing in return) .
■Client must perform an ongoing self-assessment in conjunction with receiving assessments from other clients and staff; these assessments require that clients be morally accountable on all levels of functioning: their beliefs, their attitudes, and virtually all their behavior .

Facilitator Training

Facilitator training sessions in MRT methods run for 32 hours and are held frequently across the United States. Sessions are offered monthly in Memphis, Tennessee, and frequently in other locations throughout the United States. For further information on training schedules, contact the *Cognitive-Behavioral Treatment Review & Moral Reconation Therapy News* at 3155 Hickory Hill Suite 104, Memphis, TN 38115, 901-360-1564; e-mail: CCIMRT@aol.com; Web sites: *www.ccimrt.com* and *www.moral-reconation-therapy.com.* Louisiana State University at Shreveport issues continuing education units for accredited trainers.

See this link for CCI MRT Facilitator Training dates and locations: https://www.ccimrt.com/product-category/training-events/

Program #4: Reasoning and Rehabilitation (R&R):

Program R&R, Part I:

Developed by Robert Ross and Elizabeth Fabiano in 1985 at the University of Ottawa, Reasoning and Rehabilitation (R&R) is a cognitive-behavioral program that, like MRT, is based on the theory that offenders suffer from cognitive and social deficits (see Ross, Fabiano, and Ross, 1986). Ross and Fabiano's research that stands as the basis for the principles of R&R was published in the text *Time to Think: A Cognitive Model of Delinquency Prevention and Offender Rehabilitation* (1985). The techniques used in this program were modified from techniques used in previous correctional programs as well as methods that the authors of this program found to be of value when used with offenders. They were field tested in an experimental study with high-risk probationers in Ontario, Canada.

The authors of this program attempted to provide a program that could be used in a broad range of institutional or community corrections settings as well as one that could be used concurrently with other programs in which offenders may participate.

They encourage significant individuals in the offender's life to be familiar with the program principles so that they can reinforce and encourage the offender in skill acquisition.

Approach

This program focuses on enhancing self-control, interpersonal problem solving, social perspectives, and prosocial attitudes (see Wilson, Bouffard, and MacKenzie, 2005). Participants are taught to think before acting, to consider consequences of actions, and to conceptualize alternate patterns of behavior. The program consists of 35 sessions, running from 8 to 12 weeks, with 6 to 8 participants. The sessions include audiovisual presentations, games, puzzles, reasoning exercises, role playing, modeling, and group discussions. The program developers sought to ensure value and appeal of the materials to offenders, thereby providing a program that is both enjoyable yet demanding.

Session topics include problem-solving techniques (e.g., information gathering, conceptualizing, alternative thinking, assertive communication), creative thinking, social skills, managing emotions, negotiation, critical reasoning, and values. Also important are learning to respond to complaints, being open minded, and responding to the feelings of others.

R&R's authors believe that highly trained professionals (e.g., psychiatrists, psychologists, social workers) may not always be the ones implementing rehabilitation programs, and therefore took steps to ensure that line staff would also be adept at implementing the program, as long as they possess the following characteristics:

■Above-average verbal skills.
■Ability to relate empathetically to offenders while maintaining rules, regulations, and the mission of the correctional agency.
■Sensitivity to group dynamics.
■Ability to confront offenders but not demean them.
■Above-average interpersonal skills.
■Successful experience managing unmotivated, hostile, or critical individuals.
■Humility and the consideration of others' views.
■Enthusiasm.
■Understanding of the cognitive model.

Trainers are encouraged to add to or modify the program to best serve specific types of offenders. The authors of this program make note of the importance of trainers presenting the material just above the functioning level of the offenders so as to be challenging, yet not overwhelming or discouraging. See Appendix for specifics regarding training, cost, and certification.

Program R&R, Part 2 (R&R2) (Shorter Version):

A shorter version of R&R, known as R&R2, is a program specifically for adults that was developed by Robert Ross and Jim Hilborn in 1996. This is a specialized, 15-session edition that seeks to target those over age 18 whose antisocial behavior led them to social services or criminal justice agencies.

The authors of this program of R&R2 believe that long-term intervention can both "tax the motivation of many offenders and [be] associated with high attrition rates"; it can also tax the motivation of trainers and overburden agency budgets (Ross and Hilborn, 2007 in press, p. 16). The authors of this program also note that evaluation reviews have concluded that the largest effects, proportionally, occur when cognitive programs are small and that shorter cognitive skills programs can be as effective as longer ones.

R&R2 is also designed to correct a shortcoming of previous versions that did not allow the program to be tailored to the needs and circumstances of the group recipients (Ross and Hilborn, 2007 in press). The new program offers specialized versions specific to age, sex, nature of the antisocial behavior, risk of recidivism, and culture.

R&R2 principles include:

■Motivational interviewing .
■Prosocial modeling .
■Relapse prevention .
■Desistance (encouragement to acquire a long-term prosocial lifestyle) .

[Trainers are encouraged to add to or modify the program to best serve specific types of offenders, so as to be challenging, yet not overwhelming or discouraging.]

■**Participant assessment.** R&R2 allows participants to experience CBT and assess whether they may be open to further program treatments.
■**Motivation.** Participants may become engaged in the process and more motivated to get involved in longer treatment programs.
■**Preparation.** Often, programs require a higher level of cognitive skills than many participants possess. R&R2 allows them to learn the skills required to continue with cognitive behavioral programs.

An IQ of approximately 70 or higher, as shown by prescreening, is necessary for participants to benefit from this training. Any severe psychopathology should be predetermined as well, so that one participant'ş disruptiveness will not interfere with the other participants' progress.

The authors of this program emphasize their consideration of the "Risk Principle"; that is, they concede that high-risk offenders' engagement with low-risk offenders within the program may provide modeling of delinquent behaviors. Separate groups for low-risk offenders are therefore important. (On the other hand, individuals who have learned more prosocial behaviors could be included with high-risk offenders to serve as role models.)

The ideal implementation of R&R2 is to teach low-risk offenders the skills to function prosocially and avoid being involved in longer programs with high-risk offenders. According to the authors of this program, the trainer's observations of the participants' performance in the shorter program may also help them identify those who are most likely to be harmed by their enrollment in programs alongside high-risk offenders.

The R&R2 program does not require participants to discuss their illegal behavior. Trainers are encouraged to redirect antisocial talk or behavior when it occurs within the group toward more acceptable and positive discussions.

The program provides just over 1,000 minutes of actual training. Lessons require the transfer of cognitive skills to real-life events, and every one of the 16 sessions has homework assignments. Each session includes time for feedback from participants on their observations and experiences that occurred between sessions. R&R2 manuals include the "Handbook," which is a detailed instruction manual for trainers that has all materials required for each session, and the "Participant's Workbook," which contains handouts, exercises, and worksheets that should be available for each participant. The ideal group size is 8 participants or, depending on the characteristics of the group, no less than 4 and no more than 10. R&R2 requires no special facilities, although an overhead projector and flip chart are needed. The manual suggests a preferred room setup. Sessions are flexible, but two to three 90-minute sessions per week are suggested. Staggering entry into the program is possible and trainers can provide new entrants with "catchup" sessions.

The authors caution that R&R2 should not be considered only an "offending behavior" or "therapeutic" program. They assert that it is an "approach to the treatment not only of criminal behavior but of a variety of antisocial behaviors" (Ross and Hilborn, 2007 in press, p. 21). It is a way of equipping antisocial individuals with the skills and attitudes necessary to help them avoid future problems or to cope with problems more effectively .

Facilitator Training

Those interested in learning to facilitate Ross and Fabiano's Reasoning and Rehabilitation R&R programs 1 or 2 are directed to the Author's: *Reasoning and Rehabilitation: A Handbook for Teaching Cognitive Skills,* T3 Associates, Ottawa, Ontario.

Program #5:   Relapse Prevention Therapy (RPT)

As described by authors George A. Parks and G. Alan Marlatt (2000), Relapse Prevention Therapy (RPT) was originally developed to be a maintenance program to prevent and manage relapse following addiction treatment. Designed to teach individuals how to anticipate and cope with relapse, RPT rejects the use of labels such as "alcoholic" or "drug addict," and encourages clients to think of their addictive behavior as something they *do* rather than something they *are.*

RPT uses techniques from cognitive-behavioral coping-skills training to teach clients self-management and self-control of their thoughts and behavior. This approach views addictive behaviors as acquired habits with "biological, psychological, and social determinants and consequences" (Marlatt, Parks, and Witkiewitz, 2002, p. 2). Since impaired judgment and loss of impulse control are often associated with alcohol and drug abuse, the program has also been used as a component in treating aggression and violent behavior (Cullen and Freeman-Longo, 2001) as well as sex offending (Laws, Hudson, and Ward, 2000). Most recently, **RPT** has been extended as a case management tool applicable to any type of criminal conduct (Parks et al., 2004).

Approach

Parks and Marlatt (2000) indicate that 75 percent of relapses, as reported by Marlatt and Donovan (2005), were due to three categories of high-risk situations: negative emotional states, interpersonal conflict, and social pressure. More recently, relapse determinants have been categorized into a total of eight types (Marlatt, Parks, and Witkiewitz, 2002). One is "Intrapersonal-Environmental Determinants," which are associated with factors within the individual and reactions to nonpersonal events. This includes coping with negative emotions, dysphoric states, and reactions to stress (exams, public speaking, financial difficulties, etc.). Another category is "Interpersonal Determinants," which includes factors surrounding the presence or influence of others, such as interpersonal conflict, frustration and anger, and social pressure (either direct or indirect).

RPT proposes that relapse is less likely to occur when an individual possesses effective coping mechanisms to deal with such high-risk situations. With this, the individual experiences increased self-efficacy and, as the length of abstinence from inappropriate behavior increases and effective coping with risk situations multiplies, the likelihood of relapse diminishes.

RPT involves five therapeutic strategies:

■Coping-skills training, which teaches ways to handle urges and cravings that occur in early stages of the habit change journey.
■"Relapse Road Maps," which are used to identify tempting and dangerous situations, with "detours" presented for avoiding these situations and successfully coping without having a lapse or relapse.
■Strategies to identify and cope with cognitive distortions, such as denial and rationalization, that can increase the possibility of relapse with little conscious awareness.

■Lifestyle modification techniques, so that alcohol or drug use is replaced with constructive and health-promoting activities and habits.
■Learning to anticipate possible relapses, with unrealistic expectations of perfection replaced with encouragement to be prepared for mistakes or breakdowns and skills taught on how to learn from those mistakes and continue on.

RPT begins with the identification of an individual's high risk for situationswhere relapse could occur and with an evaluation of his or her ability to cope with those situations. In-depth programs of change are necessary because it is impossible to identify all the possibilities for high-risk situations for any one client. Marlatt, Parks, and Witkiewitz (2002) identified two additional required aspects: helping clients create a balanced lifestyle to increase their capacity to deal with stress and, therefore, increase self-efficacy; and teaching an identification process toward early warning signs of high-risk situations and ways to evoke self-control strategies to prevent relapse.

In summary, RPT clients are taught to:

■Understand relapse as a process, not an event.
■Identify and cope with high-risk situations.
■Cope effectively with urges and cravings.
■Implement damage control procedures during lapses to minimize their negative consequences and get back on the road to recovery.
■Stay engaged in treatment, particularly after relapses occur.
■Create a more balanced lifestyle.

Facilitator Training

Workshops of **1** to 5 days are offered by the Addictive Behaviors Research Center at the University of Washington in Seattle. Programs focus on several key themes and are flexible to meet the needs of different organizations and trainees. Topics include Cognitive-Behavioral Therapy for Offenders 101, Cognitive-Behavioral Offender Substance Abuse Treatment, Relapse Prevention with Offenders, Integrated Treatment of Co-Occurring Disorders, Offender Re-Entry Planning, and Relapse Prevention as an Offender Case Management Tool.

Consultation and technical assistance on implementing Cognitive-Behavioral Programs is also available. Contact George A. Parks, Ph.D., Department of Psychology, Box 351629, University of Washington, Seattle, WA 98195-1629,206-685-7504.

Program #6:   Thinking For A Change (T4C):

In December 1997, the National Institute of Corrections (NIC) introduced a new integrated cognitive-behavioral change program for offenders and sought a limited number of local, state, or federal correctional agencies to serve as field test sites for the program, Thinking for a Change (T4C). An overwhelming response from the corrections community requesting participation in the project necessitated immediate program expansion and the inclusion of a much broader scope of participation for the field test. Since its introduction, correctional agencies in more than 40 states have implemented T4C with offender populations. These agencies include state correctional systems, local jails, community-based corrections programs, and probation and parole departments. The offender populations included in the project represent both adults and juveniles and males and females. More than 5,000 correctional staff have been trained to facilitate offender groups. Nearly 500 individuals have participated in Thinking for a Change: Advanced Practicum (Training of Trainers), which enables participants to train additional facilitators at their agencies to deliver the program. As research of the effectiveness of the program continues to mount, so does the interest from the correctional community to adopt a quality, evidenced-based cognitive-behavioral change program.

Approach

T4C (Bush, Glick, and Taymans, 1997) uses a combination of approaches to increase offenders' awareness of self and others. It integrates cognitive restructuring, social skills, and problem solving. The program begins by teaching offenders an introspective process for examining their ways of thinking and their feelings, beliefs, and attitudes. This process is reinforced throughout the program. Social-skills training is provided as an alternative to antisocial behaviors. The program culminates by integrating the skills offenders have learned into steps for problem solving. Problem solving becomes the central approach offenders learn that enables them to work through difficult situations without engaging in criminal behavior.

Offenders learn how to report on situations that could lead to criminal behavior and to identify the cognitive processes that might lead them to offending. They learn how to write and use a "thinking report" as a means of determining their awareness of the risky thinking that leads them into trouble. Within the social skills component of the program, offenders try using their newly developed social skills in role-playing situations. After each role-play, the group discusses and assesses how well the participant did in following the steps of the social skill being learned. Offenders also apply problem-solving steps to problems in their own lives. Written homework assignments, a social skills checklist, and input from a person who knows the participant well are all used by the class to create a profile of necessary social skills, which becomes the basis for additional lessons. Through a variety of approaches, including cognitive restructuring, social-skills training, and problem solving, T4C seeks to provide offenders with the skills as well as the internal motivation necessary to avoid criminal be behavior.

The broad spectrum of the program's sessions makes T4C meaningful for a variety of offenders, including adults and juveniles, probationers, prison and jail inmates, and those in aftercare or on parole. A brief 15-minute prescreening session to reinforce the participant's need for the program and the necessity of positive participation is the first step in T4C. Small groups of 8 to 12 individuals are encouraged in order to facilitate interactive and productive feedback. The program can be used concurrently or consecutively with other treatment programs.

The curriculum is divided into 22 lessons, each lasting 1 to 2 hours. No more than one lesson should be offered per day; two per week is optimal. It is recommended that at least 10 additional sessions be held using the social skills profile developed by the class (as noted above). Lessons are sequential, and program flow and integrity are important; however, in situations of high turnover or movement to other facilities, some sessions can be used as points to reorganize or combine existing groups, freeing up one facilitator to work with a new set of offenders.

Facilitator Training

Training for facilitators of T4C is readily available on the NIC Web site, but only for Bureau Of Prisons Employees and Approved Government Contractors, earmarked to deliver these programs. For the rest of the civilian population it is required to attend the seminar in person.

Overview of Thinking for a Change

■Twenty-two lessons with capacity to extend program indefinitely.
■Additional 10 lessons recommended for participants to explore self-evaluations done in the 22nd lesson.
■One to two hours weekly.
■Facilitators need not have any specific credential or level of education, but must:
■Be caring.
■Like to teach.
■Understand group processes and interpersonal interactions .
■Be able to control an offender group .
■Be trained in a 3- to 5-day T4C implementation plan with two master trainers .
■Lesson format: Understand, learn, perform .
■Homework review .
■Summary and rationale for the specific lesson .
■Definition of words and concepts .

■Activities:

- Skits .
- Modeling .
- Feedback.
- Overheads .
- Handouts .
- Pocket cards .

Delivery Of The T4C Program Manual

■*A Manual for Delivery of Cognitive Self Change* (written by Jack Bush of the Vermont Department of Corrections, 2012):

- The Manual for Delivery of Cognitive Self Change is an *in-depth guide to utilization of the T4C program* and includes an overview of Cognitive Self Change, the Thinking Report, Cognitive Check-Ins; delivery of the program, case management, program standards, and administrative procedures; admission, discharge, and transfer procedures; group delivery, program management, and supervision; and helpful forms and program memoranda.

■Thinking for a Change: Facilitator Training: Lesson Plans (developed by T4C creators Jack Bush, Barry Glick, and Juliana Taymans, 2001) is a 32-hour training program designed to teach the theoretical foundations of CBT and specifically the basic components of T4C, including cognitive self-change, social skills, problem solving, and implementation of the program.

Engaging In Productive Activities For Earned Time Credits:

Productive activities earned time credits are available for an inmate who enjoys at least

one low or minimal recidivism risk assessment, for a credit of 10 days out of 30 days earnestly

spent in productive activities while incarcerated. For those inmates who achieve a second

subsequent low or minimal recidivism risk assessment, the time credit increases an additional 5

days, bringing the total earned time credit up to 15 days for every 30 days earnestly spent in

productive activities while incarcerated. This is quite an incentive for signing up for and successfully completing productive activities, that can either be group activities or individual activities.

18 U.S. Code § 3635(3)(2019) sets forth a "list" of activities the Congress considered to be either recidivism reduction and/or productive activities that an inmate could engage in for earned time credits. The list is quite expansive. Attorney General Barr intends to release a list of approved productive activities for First Step Act Of 2018 implementation in January, 2018. The list will almost certainly include correspondence courses through the mail, as the Bureau Of Prisons has permitted inmates to engage in college correspondence courses for years, and because this activity is clearly productive for the inmate.

Academic Classes - Correspondence College Courses Examined Here:

¶ (iv.) of 18 U.S. Code § 3635(3)(2019) states that "academic classes" are considered productive activities. The Bureau Of Prisons permits federal inmates to sign up for correspondence college classes, that can be either degree programs, or individual courses, for earned time credits. For those that do not have a GED, the Bureau Of Prisons provides programs to earn a GED first. Regarding through the mail (not online) college programs or courses, there are several United States based accredited colleges that offer college course work for inmates. This is an enormous step in the right direction for prison reform. The State Of Colorado appears to be ahead of the bell shaped curve on prison reform activities related to correspondence college programs and courses, as Colorado is home to two out of the three accredited colleges listed below.

1. **Adams State University** in Colorado offers a diverse choice of courses and programs available, is accredited, and was probably the first college in the country to embrace correspondence college for inmates. Adams offers both undergraduate and advanced college degrees for inmates, completely through the mail. https://www.adams.edu/academics/print-based/prison-college-program/

2. **Upper Iowa University (UIU)** in Iowa offers a diverse choice of courses, as well as all types of college courses and self paced degree programs. https://www.adams.edu/academics/print-based/prison-college-program/

3. **Colorado State University Pueblo** offers independent studies correspondence program choices, with 100+ college courses to choose from. This is a State University and a great choice. https://www.csupueblo.edu/extended-studies/independent-study/index.html

Although the Bureau Of Prisons will not pay for an inmate's college tuition, correspondence

college courses appear to be quite reasonable, between $600-$1,000 per course. When coupled with

the potential for earned productive activities time credits over an extended period of time,

correspondence college is a worthwhile investment for any inmate that wants to better themselves

through self study, while earning productive activity time credits for early release. This is an individual

activity within the tenets of the First Step Act Of 2018 that should be strongly considered as a basis to

earn productive activity early release time credits, while staying at a low or minimal recidivism

assessment status through multiple recidivism risk assessments.

The First Step Act Of 2018 (Reformatted Text) For Easy Reading Follows

[This space intentionally left blank]

ONE HUNDRED FIFTEENTH
CONGRESS OF THE UNITED STATES
OF AMERICA 2D SESSION

Begun and held at the City of Washington on Wednesday, the third day of January, two thousand and eighteen

S. 756

AN ACT

To reauthorize and amend the Marine Debris Act to promote international action to reduce marine debris, and for other purposes.

Section 1. Short title; table of contents

(a) Short title.—

This Act may be cited as the "First Step Act of 2018".

(b) Table of contents.—

The table of contents for this Act is as follows:

Sec. 1. Short title; table of contents.

TITLE I—Recidivism reduction

Sec. 101. Risk and needs assessment system.
Sec. 102. Implementation of system and recommendations by Bureau of Prisons.
Sec. 103. GAO report.
Sec. 104. Authorization of appropriations. Sec.

Sec. 105. Rule of construction.

Sec. 106. Faith-based considerations.

Sec. 107. Independent Review Committee.

TITLE II—Bureau of Prisons secure firearms storage

Sec. 201. Short title.

Sec. 202. Secure firearms storage.

TITLE III—Restraints on pregnant prisoners prohibited

Sec. 301. Use of restraints on prisoners during the period of pregnancy and postpartum recovery prohibited.

TITLE IV—Sentencing reform

Sec. 401. Reduce and restrict enhanced sentencing for prior drug felonies. Sec.

Sec. 402. Broadening of existing safety valve.

Sec. 403. Clarification of section 924(c) of title 18, United States Code.

Sec. 404. Application of Fair Sentencing Act.

TITLE V—Second Chance Act of 2007 reauthorization

Sec. 501. Short title.

Sec. 502. Improvements to existing programs.

Sec. 503. Audit and accountability of grantees.

Sec. 504. Federal reentry improvements.

Sec. 505. Federal interagency reentry coordination. Sec.

Sec. 506. Conference expenditures.

Sec. 507. Evaluation of the Second Chance Act program.

Sec. 508. GAO review.

TITLE VI—Miscellaneous criminal justice

Sec. 601. Placement of prisoners close to families. Sec.

Sec. 602. Home confinement for low-risk prisoners.

Sec. 603. Federal prisoner reentry initiative reauthorization; modification of imposed term of imprisonment.

Sec. 604. Identification for returning citizens.

Sec. 605. Expanding inmate employment through Federal Prison Industries. Sec.

Sec. 606. De-escalation training.

Sec. 607. Evidence-Based treatment for opioid and heroin abuse.

Sec. 608. Pilot programs.

Sec. 609. Ensuring supervision of released sexually dangerous persons. Sec.

Sec. 610. Data collection.

Sec. 611. Healthcare products.

Sec. 612. Adult and juvenile collaboration programs. Sec.

Sec. 613. Juvenile solitary confinement.

Title I

Recidivism reduction

Sec. 101. Risk and needs assessment system

(a) In general.—

Chapter 229 of title 18, United States Code, is amended by inserting after subchapter C the following:

Subchapter D

Risk and Needs Assessment System

Sec.
3631. Duties of the Attorney General.
3632. Development of risk and needs assessment system.
3633. Evidence-based recidivism reduction program and recommendations. 3634. Report.
3635. Definitions.

Sec. 3631. Duties of the Attorney General

(a) In general.—

The Attorney General shall carry out this subchapter in consultation with—

(1) the Director of the Bureau of Prisons;

(2) the Director of the Administrative Office of the United States Courts;

(3) the Director of the Office of Probation and Pretrial Services;

(4) the Director of the National Institute of Justice;

(5) the Director of the National Institute of Corrections; and

(6) the Independent Review Committee authorized by the First Step Act of 2018.

(b) Duties.—

The Attorney General shall—

(1) conduct a review of the existing prisoner risk and needs assessment systems in operation on the date of enactment of this subchapter;

(2) develop recommendations regarding evidence-based recidivism reduction programs and productive activities in accordance with section 3633;

(3) conduct ongoing research and data analysis on—

(A) evidence-based recidivism reduction programs relating to the use of prisoner risk and needs assessment tools;

(B) the most effective and efficient uses of such programs;

(C) which evidence-based recidivism reduction programs are the most effective at reducing recidivism, and the type, amount, and intensity of programming that most effectively reduces the risk of recidivism; and

(D) products purchased by Federal agencies that are manufactured overseas and could be manufactured by prisoners participating in a prison work program without reducing job opportunities for other workers in the United States;

(4) on an annual basis, review, validate, and release publicly on the Department of Justice website the risk and needs assessment system, which review shall include—

(A) any subsequent changes to the risk and needs assessment system made after the date of enactment of this subchapter;

(B) the recommendations developed under paragraph (2), using the research conducted under paragraph (3);

(C) an evaluation to ensure that the risk and needs assessment system bases the assessment of each prisoner's risk of recidivism on indicators of progress and of regression that are dynamic and that can reasonably be expected to change while in prison;

(D) statistical validation of any tools that the risk and needs assessment system uses; and

(E) an evaluation of the rates of recidivism among similarly classified prisoners to identify any unwarranted disparities, including disparities among similarly classified prisoners of different demographic groups, in such rates;

(5) make any revisions or updates to the risk and needs assessment system that the Attorney General determines appropriate pursuant to the review under paragraph (4), including updates to ensure that any disparities identified in paragraph (4)(E) are reduced to the greatest extent possible; and

(6) report to Congress in accordance with section 3634.

Sec. 3632. Development of risk and needs assessment system

(a) In general.—

Not later than 210 days after the date of enactment of this subchapter, the Attorney General, in consultation with the Independent Review Committee authorized by the First Step Act of 2018, shall develop and release publicly on the Department of Justice website a risk and needs assessment system (referred to in this subchapter as the "System"), which shall be used to—

(1) determine the recidivism risk of each prisoner as part of the intake process, and classify each prisoner as having minimum, low, medium, or high risk for recidivism;

(2) assess and determine, to the extent practicable, the risk of violent or serious misconduct of each prisoner;

(3) determine the type and amount of evidence-based recidivism reduction programming that is appropriate for each prisoner and assign each prisoner to such programming accordingly, and based on the prisoner's specific criminogenic needs, and in accordance with subsection (b);

(4) reassess the recidivism risk of each prisoner periodically, based on factors including indicators of progress, and of regression, that are dynamic and that can reasonably be expected to change while in prison;

(5) reassign the prisoner to appropriate evidence-based recidivism reduction programs or productive activities based on the revised determination to ensure that—

(A) all prisoners at each risk level have a meaningful opportunity to reduce their classification during the period of incarceration;

(B) to address the specific criminogenic needs of the prisoner; and

(C) all prisoners are able to successfully participate in such programs;

(6) determine when to provide incentives and rewards for successful participation in evidence-based recidivism reduction programs or productive activities in accordance with subsection (e);

(7) determine when a prisoner is ready to transfer into prerelease custody or supervised release in accordance with section 3624; and

(8) determine the appropriate use of audio technology for program course materials with an understanding of dyslexia.

In carrying out this subsection, the Attorney General may use existing risk and needs assessment tools, as appropriate.

(b) Assignment of evidence-based recidivism reduction programs.—

The System shall provide guidance on the type, amount, and intensity of evidence-based recidivism reduction programming and productive activities that shall be assigned for each prisoner, including—

(1) programs in which the Bureau of Prisons shall assign the prisoner to participate, according to the prisoner's specific criminogenic needs; and

(2) information on the best ways that the Bureau of Prisons can tailor the programs to the specific criminogenic needs of each prisoner so as to most effectively lower each prisoner's risk of recidivism.

(c) Housing and assignment decisions.—

The System shall provide guidance on program grouping and housing assignment determinations and, after accounting for the safety of each prisoner and other individuals at the prison, provide that prisoners with a similar risk level be grouped together in housing and assignment decisions to the extent practicable.

(d) Evidence-Based recidivism reduction program incentives and productive activities rewards.—

The System shall provide incentives and rewards for prisoners to participate in and complete evidence-based recidivism reduction programs as follows:

(1) Phone and visitation privileges.—

A prisoner who is successfully participating in an evidence-based recidivism reduction program shall receive—

(A) phone privileges, or, if available, video conferencing privileges, for up to 30 minutes per day, and up to 510 minutes per month; and

(B) additional time for visitation at the prison, as determined by the warden of the prison.

(2) Transfer to institution closer to release residence.—

A prisoner who is successfully participating in an evidence-based recidivism reduction program shall be considered by the Bureau of Prisons for placement in a facility closer to the prisoner's release residence upon request from the prisoner and subject to—

(A) bed availability at the transfer facility;

(B) the prisoner's security designation; and

(C) the recommendation from the warden of the prison at which the prisoner is incarcerated at the time of making the request.

(3) Additional policies.—

The Director of the Bureau of Prisons shall develop additional policies to provide appropriate incentives for successful participation and completion of evidence-based recidivism reduction programming. The incentives shall include not less than 2 of the following:

(A) Increased commissary spending limits and product offerings.

(B) Extended opportunities to access the email system.

(C) Consideration of transfer to preferred housing units (including transfer to different prison facilities).

(D) Other incentives solicited from prisoners and determined appropriate by the Director.

(4) Time credits.—

(A) In general.—

A prisoner, except for an ineligible prisoner under subparagraph (D), who successfully completes evidence-based recidivism reduction programming or productive activities, shall earn time credits as follows:

(i) A prisoner shall earn 10 days of time credits for every 30 days of successful participation in evidence-based recidivism reduction programming or productive activities.

(ii) A prisoner determined by the Bureau of Prisons to be at a minimum or low risk for recidivating, who, over 2 consecutive assessments, has not increased their risk of recidivism, shall earn an additional 5 days of time credits for every 30 days of successful participation in evidence-based recidivism reduction programming or productive activities.

(B) Availability.—

A prisoner may not earn time credits under this paragraph for an evidence-based recidivism reduction program that the prisoner successfully completed—

(i) prior to the date of enactment of this subchapter; or

(ii) during official detention prior to the date that the prisoner's sentence commences under section 3585(a).

(C) Application of time credits toward prerelease custody or supervised release.—

Time credits earned under this paragraph by prisoners who successfully participate in recidivism reduction programs or productive activities shall be applied toward time in prerelease custody or supervised release. The Director of the Bureau of Prisons shall transfer eligible prisoners, as determined under section 3624(g), into prerelease custody or supervised release.

(D) Ineligible prisoners.—

A prisoner is ineligible to receive time credits under this paragraph if the prisoner is serving a sentence for a conviction under any of the following provisions of law:

(i) Section 32, relating to destruction of aircraft or aircraft facilities.

(ii) Section 33, relating to destruction of motor vehicles or motor vehicle facilities.

(iii) Section 36, relating to drive-by shootings.

(iv) Section 81, relating to arson within special maritime and territorial jurisdiction.

(v) Section 111(b), relating to assaulting, resisting, or impeding certain officers or employees using a deadly or dangerous weapon or inflicting bodily injury.

(vi) Paragraph (1), (7), or (8) of section 113(a), relating to assault with intent to commit murder, assault resulting in substantial bodily injury to a spouse or intimate partner, a dating partner, or an individual who has not attained the age of 16 years, or assault of a spouse, intimate partner, or dating partner by strangling, suffocating, or attempting to strangle or suffocate.

(vii) Section 115, relating to influencing, impeding, or retaliating against a Federal official by injuring a family member, except for a threat made in violation of that section.

(viii) Section 116, relating to female genital mutilation.

(ix) Section 117, relating to domestic assault by a habitual offender.

(x) Any section of chapter 10, relating to biological weapons.

(xi) Any section of chapter 11B, relating to chemical weapons.

(xii) Section 351, relating to Congressional, Cabinet, and Supreme Court assassination, kidnapping, and assault.

(xiii) Section 521, relating to criminal street gangs.

(xiv) Section 751, relating to prisoners in custody of an institution or officer.

(xv) Section 793, relating to gathering, transmitting, or losing defense information.

(xvi) Section 794, relating to gathering or delivering defense information to aid a foreign government.

(xvii) Any section of chapter 39, relating to explosives and other dangerous articles, except for section 836 (relating to the transportation of fireworks into a State prohibiting sale or use).

(xviii) Section 842(p), relating to distribution of information relating to explosives, destructive devices, and weapons of mass destruction, but only if the conviction involved a weapon of mass destruction (as defined in section 2332a(c)).

(xix) Subsection (f)(3), (h), or (i) of section 844, relating to the use of fire or an explosive.

(xx) Section 871, relating to threats against the President and successors to the Presidency.

(xxi) Section 879, relating to threats against former Presidents and certain other persons.

(xxii) Section 924(c), relating to unlawful possession or use of a firearm during and in relation to any crime of violence or drug trafficking crime.

(xxiii) Section 1030(a)(1), relating to fraud and related activity in connection with computers.

(xxiv) Section 1091, relating to genocide.

(xxv) Any section of chapter 51, relating to homicide, except for section 1112 (relating to manslaughter), 1113 (relating to attempt to commit murder or manslaughter, but only if the conviction was for an attempt to commit manslaughter), 1115 (relating to misconduct or neglect of ship officers), or 1122 (relating to protection against the human immunodeficiency virus).

(xxvi) Any section of chapter 55, relating to kidnapping.

(xxvii) Any offense under chapter 77, relating to peonage, slavery, and trafficking in persons, except for sections 1593 through 1596.

(xxviii) Section 1751, relating to Presidential and Presidential staff assassination, kidnapping, and assault.

(xxix) Section 1791, relating to providing or possessing contraband in prison.

(xxx) Section 1792, relating to mutiny and riots.

(xxxi) Section 1841(a)(2)(C), relating to intentionally killing or attempting to kill an unborn child.

(xxxii) Section 1992, relating to terrorist attacks and other violence against railroad carriers and against mass transportation systems on land, on water, or through the air.

(xxxiii) Section 2113(e), relating to bank robbery resulting in death.

(xxxiv) Section 2118(c), relating to robberies and burglaries involving controlled substances resulting in assault, putting in jeopardy the life of any person by the use of a dangerous weapon or device, or death.

(xxxv) Section 2119, relating to taking a motor vehicle (commonly referred to as "carjacking").

(xxxvi) Any section of chapter 105, relating to sabotage, except for section 2152.

(xxxvii) Any section of chapter 109A, relating to sexual abuse.

(xxxviii) Section 2250, relating to failure to register as a sex offender.

(xxxix) Section 2251, relating to the sexual exploitation of children.

(xl) Section 2251A, relating to the selling or buying of children.

(xli) Section 2252, relating to certain activities relating to

material involving the sexual exploitation of minors.

(xlii) Section 2252A, relating to certain activities involving material constituting or containing child pornography.

(xliii) Section 2260, relating to the production of sexually explicit depictions of a minor for importation into the United States.

(xliv) Section 2283, relating to the transportation of explosive, biological, chemical, or radioactive or nuclear materials.

(xlv) Section 2284, relating to the transportation of terrorists.

(xlvi) Section 2291, relating to the destruction of a vessel or maritime facility, but only if the conduct that led to the conviction involved a substantial risk of death or serious bodily injury.

(xlvii) Any section of chapter 113B, relating to terrorism.

(xlviii) Section 2340A, relating to torture.

(xlix) Section 2381, relating to treason.

(l) Section 2442, relating to the recruitment or use of child soldiers.

(li) An offense described in section 3559(c)(2)(F), for which the offender was sentenced to a term of imprisonment of more than 1 year, if the offender has a previous conviction, for which the offender served a term of imprisonment of more than 1 year, for a Federal or State offense, by whatever designation and wherever committed, consisting of murder (as described in section 1111), voluntary manslaughter (as described in section 1112), assault with intent to commit murder (as described in section 113(a)), aggravated sexual abuse and sexual abuse (as described in sections 2241 and 2242), abusive sexual contact (as described in sections 2244(a)(1) and (a)(2)), kidnapping (as described in chapter 55), carjacking (as described in section 2119), arson (as described in section 844(f)(3), (h), or (i)), or terrorism (as described in chapter 113B).

(lii) Section 57(b) of the Atomic Energy Act of 1954 (42 U.S.C. 2077(b) (https://www.law.cornell.edu/uscode/text/42/2077#b)), relating to the engagement or participation in the development or production of special nuclear material.

(liii) Section 92 of the Atomic Energy Act of 1954 (42 U.S.C. 2122 (https://www.law.cornell.edu/uscode/text/42/2122)), relating to prohibitions governing atomic weapons.

(liv) Section 101 of the Atomic Energy Act of 1954 (42 U.S.C. 2131 (https://www.law.cornell.edu/uscode/text/42/2131)), relating to the atomic energy license requirement.

(lv) Section 224 or 225 of the Atomic Energy Act of 1954 (42 U.S.C. 2274 (https://www.law.cornell.edu/uscode/text/42/2274), 2275), relating to the communication or receipt of restricted data.

(lvi) Section 236 of the Atomic Energy Act of 1954 (42 U.S.C. 2284 (https://www.law.cornell.edu/uscode/text/42/2284)), relating to the sabotage of nuclear facilities or fuel.

(lvii) Section 60123(b) of title 49 (https://www.law.cornell.edu/uscode/text/49/60123#b), relating to damaging or destroying a pipeline facility, but only if the conduct which led to the conviction involved a substantial risk of death or serious bodily injury.

(lviii) Section 401(a) of the Controlled Substances Act (21 U.S.C. 841 (https://www.law.cornell.edu/uscode/text/21/841)), relating to manufacturing or distributing a controlled substance in the case of a conviction for an offense described in subparagraph (A), (B), or (C) of subsection (b)(1) of that section for which death or serious bodily injury resulted from the use of such substance.

(lix) Section 276(a) of the Immigration and Nationality Act (8 U.S.C. 1326 (https://www.law.cornell.edu/uscode/text/8/1326)), relating to the reentry of a removed alien, but only if the alien is described in paragraph (1) or (2) of subsection (b) of that section.

(lx) Section 277 of the Immigration and Nationality Act (8 U.S.C. 1327 (https://www.law.cornell.edu/uscode/text/8/1327)), relating to aiding or assisting certain aliens to enter the United States.

(lxi) Section 278 of the Immigration and Nationality Act (8 U.S.C. 1328 (https://www.law.cornell.edu/uscode/text/8/1328)), relating to the importation of an alien into the United States for an immoral purpose.

(lxii) Any section of the Export Administration Act of 1979 (50 U.S.C. 4611 (https://www.law.cornell.edu/uscode/text/50/4611) et seq.)

(lxiii) Section 206 of the International Emergency Economic Powers Act (50 U.S.C. 1705 (https://www.law.cornell.edu/uscode/text/50/1705)).

(lxiv) Section 601 of the National Security Act of 1947 (50 U.S.C. 3121 (https://www.law.cornell.edu/uscode/text/50/3121)), relating to the protection of identities of certain United States undercover intelligence officers, agents, informants, and sources.

(lxv) Subparagraph (A)(i) or (B)(i) of section 401(b)(1) of the Controlled Substances Act (21 U.S.C. 841(b)(1) (https://www.law.cornell.edu/uscode/text/21/841#b_1)) or paragraph (1)(A) or (2)(A) of section 1010(b) of the Controlled Substances Import and Export Act (21 U.S.C. 960(b) (https://www.law.cornell.edu/uscode/text/21/960#b)), relating to manufacturing, distributing, dispensing, or possessing with intent to manufacture, distribute, dispense, or knowingly importing or exporting, a mixture or substance containing a detectable amount of heroin if the sentencing court finds that the offender was an organizer, leader, manager, or supervisor of others in the offense, as determined under the guidelines promulgated by the United States Sentencing Commission.

(lxvi) Subparagraph (A)(vi) or (B)(vi) of section 401(b)(1) of the Controlled Substances Act (21 U.S.C. 841(b)(1) (https://www.law.cornell.edu/uscode/text/21/841#b_1)) or paragraph (1)(F) or (2)(F) of section 1010(b) of the Controlled Substances Import and Export Act (21 U.S.C. 960(b) (https://www.law.cornell.edu/uscode/text/21/960#b)), relating to manufacturing, distributing, dispensing, or possessing with intent to manufacture, distribute, or dispense, a mixture or substance containing a detectable amount of N-phenyl-N-[1-(2-phenylethyl) -4-piperidinyl] propanamide, or any analogue thereof.

(lxvii) Subparagraph (A)(viii) or (B)(viii) of section 401(b)(1) of the Controlled Substances Act (21 U.S.C. 841(b)(1) (https://www.law.cornell.edu/uscode/text/21/841#b_1)) or paragraph (1)(H) or (2)(H) of section 1010(b) the Controlled Substances Import and Export Act (21 U.S.C. 960(b) (https://www.law.cornell.edu/uscode/text/21/960#b)), relating to manufacturing, distributing, dispensing, or possessing with intent to manufacture, distribute, or dispense, or knowingly importing or exporting, a mixture of substance containing a detectable amount of methamphetamine, its salts, isomers, or salts of its isomers, if the sentencing court finds that the offender was an organizer, leader, manager, or supervisor of others in the offense, as determined under the guidelines promulgated by the United States Sentencing Commission.

(lxviii) Subparagraph (A) or (B) of section 401(b)(1) of the Controlled Substances Act (21 U.S.C. 841(b)(1) (https://www.law.cornell.edu/uscode/text/21/841#b_1)) or paragraph (1) or (2) of section 1010(b) of the Controlled Substances Import and Export Act (21 U.S.C. 960(b) (https://www.law.cornell.edu/uscode/text/21/960#b)), relating to manufacturing, distributing, dispensing, or possessing with intent to manufacture, distribute, or dispense, a controlled substance, or knowingly importing or exporting a controlled substance, if the sentencing court finds that—

    (I) the offense involved a mixture or substance containing a detectable amount of N-phenyl-N-[1-(2-phenylethyl)-4-piperidinyl] propanamide, or any analogue thereof; and

    (II) the offender was an organizer, leader, manager, or supervisor of others in the offense, as determined under the guidelines promulgated by the United States Sentencing Commission.

(E) Deportable prisoners ineligible to apply time credits.—

    (i) In general.—

A prisoner is ineligible to apply time credits under subparagraph (C) if the prisoner is the subject of a final order of removal under any provision of the immigration laws (as such term is defined in section 101(a)(17) of the Immigration and Nationality Act (8 U.S.C. 1101(a)(17) (https://www.law.cornell.edu/uscode/text/8/1101#a_17))).

    (ii) Proceedings.—

The Attorney General, in consultation with the Secretary of Homeland Security, shall ensure that any alien described in section 212 or 237 of the Immigration and Nationality Act (8 U.S.C. 1182 (https://www.law.cornell.edu/uscode/text/8/1182), 1227) who seeks to earn time credits are subject to proceedings described in section 238(a) of that Act (8 U.S.C. 1228(a) (https://www.law.cornell.edu/uscode/text/8/1228#a)) at a date as early as practicable during the prisoner's incarceration.

(5) Risk reassessments and level adjustment.—

A prisoner who successfully participates in evidence-based recidivism reduction programming or productive activities shall receive periodic risk reassessments not less often than annually, and a prisoner determined to be at a medium or high risk of recidivating and who has less than 5 years until his or her projected release date shall receive more frequent risk reassessments. If the reassessment shows that the prisoner's risk of recidivating or specific needs have changed, the Bureau of Prisons shall update the determination of the prisoner's risk of recidivating or information regarding the prisoner's specific needs and reassign the prisoner to appropriate evidence-based recidivism reduction programming or productive activities based on such changes.

(6) Relation to other incentive programs. —

The incentives described in this subsection shall be in addition to any other rewards or incentives for which a prisoner may be eligible.

(e) Penalties. —

The Director of the Bureau of Prisons shall develop guidelines for the reduction of rewards and incentives earned under subsection (d) for prisoners who violate prison rules or evidence-based recidivism reduction program or productive activity rules, which shall provide—

(1) general levels of violations and resulting reductions;

(2) that any reduction that includes the loss of time credits shall require written notice to the prisoner, shall be limited to time credits that a prisoner earned as of the date of the prisoner's rule violation, and shall not include any future time credits that the prisoner may earn; and

(3) for a procedure to restore time credits that a prisoner lost as a result of a rule violation, based on the prisoner's individual progress after the date of the rule violation.

(f) Bureau of Prisons training. —

The Attorney General shall develop and implement training programs for Bureau of Prisons officers and employees responsible for administering the System, which shall include—

(1) initial training to educate officers and employees on how to use the System in an appropriate and consistent manner, as well as the reasons for using the System;

(2) continuing education;

(3) periodic training updates; and

(4) a requirement that such officers and employees demonstrate competence in administering the System, including interrater reliability, on a biannual basis.

(g) Quality assurance.—

In order to ensure that the Bureau of Prisons is using the System in an appropriate and consistent manner, the Attorney General shall monitor and assess the use of the System, which shall include conducting annual audits of the Bureau of Prisons regarding the use of the System.

(h) Dyslexia screening.—

(1) Screening.—

The Attorney General shall incorporate a dyslexia screening program into the System, including by screening for dyslexia during—

(A) the intake process; and

(B) each periodic risk reassessment of a prisoner.

(2) Treatment.—

The Attorney General shall incorporate programs designed to treat dyslexia into the evidence-based recidivism reduction programs or productive activities required to be implemented under this section. The Attorney General may also incorporate programs designed to treat other learning disabilities.

Sec. 3633. Evidence-based recidivism reduction program and recommendations

(a) In general.—

Prior to releasing the System, in consultation with the Independent Review Committee authorized by the First Step Act of 2018, the Attorney General shall—

(1) review the effectiveness of evidence-based recidivism reduction programs that exist as of the date of enactment of this subchapter in prisons operated by the Bureau of Prisons;

(2) review available information regarding the effectiveness of evidence-based recidivism reduction programs and productive activities that exist in State-operated prisons throughout the United States;

(3) identify the most effective evidence-based recidivism reduction programs;

(4) review the policies for entering into evidence-based recidivism reduction partnerships described in section 3621(h)(5); and

(5) direct the Bureau of Prisons regarding—

   (A) evidence-based recidivism reduction programs;
   (B) the ability for faith-based organizations to function as a provider of educational evidence-based programs outside of the religious classes and services provided through the Chaplaincy; and

   (C) the addition of any new effective evidence-based recidivism reduction programs that the Attorney General finds.

(b) Review and recommendations regarding dyslexia mitigation.—

In carrying out subsection (a), the Attorney General shall consider the prevalence and mitigation of dyslexia in prisons, including by—

(1) reviewing statistics on the prevalence of dyslexia, and the effectiveness of any programs implemented to mitigate the effects of dyslexia, in prisons operated by the Bureau of Prisons and State-operated prisons throughout the United States; and

(2) incorporating the findings of the Attorney General under paragraph (1) of this subsection into any directives given to the Bureau of Prisons under paragraph (5) of subsection (a).

Sec. 3634. Report

Beginning on the date that is 2 years after the date of enactment of this subchapter, and annually thereafter for a period of 5 years, the Attorney General shall submit a report to the Committees on the Judiciary of the Senate and the House of Representatives and the Subcommittees on Commerce, Justice, Science, and Related Agencies of the Committees on Appropriations of the Senate and the House of Representatives that contains the following:

(1) A summary of the activities and accomplishments of the Attorney General in carrying out this Act.

(2) A summary and assessment of the types and effectiveness of the evidence- based recidivism reduction programs and productive activities in prisons operated by the Bureau of Prisons, including—

    (A) evidence about which programs have been shown to reduce recidivism;

    (B) the capacity of each program and activity at each prison, including the number of prisoners along with the recidivism risk of each prisoner enrolled in each program; and

    (C) identification of any gaps or shortages in capacity of such programs and activities.

(3) Rates of recidivism among individuals who have been released from Federal prison, based on the following criteria:

    (A) The primary offense of conviction.

    (B) The length of the sentence imposed and served.

    (C) The Bureau of Prisons facility or facilities in which the prisoner's sentence was served.

    (D) The evidence-based recidivism reduction programming that the prisoner successfully completed, if any.

    (E) The prisoner's assessed and reassessed risk of recidivism.

    (F) The productive activities that the prisoner successfully completed, if any.

(4) The status of prison work programs at facilities operated by the Bureau of Prisons, including—

    (A) a strategy to expand the availability of such programs without reducing job opportunities for workers in the United States who are not in the custody of the Bureau of Prisons, including the feasibility of prisoners manufacturing products purchased by Federal agencies that are manufactured overseas;

    (B) an assessment of the feasibility of expanding such programs, consistent with the strategy required under subparagraph (A), with the goal that 5 years after the date of enactment of this subchapter, not less than 75 percent of eligible minimum- and low-risk offenders have the opportunity to participate in a prison work program for not less than 20 hours per week; and

(C) a detailed discussion of legal authorities that would be useful or necessary to achieve the goals described in subparagraphs (A) and (B).

(5) An assessment of the Bureau of Prisons' compliance with section 3621(h).

(6) An assessment of progress made toward carrying out the purposes of this subchapter, including any savings associated with—

(A) the transfer of prisoners into prerelease custody or supervised release under section 3624(g), including savings resulting from the avoidance or deferral of future construction, acquisition, and operations costs; and

(B) any decrease in recidivism that may be attributed to the System or the increase in evidence-based recidivism reduction programs required under this subchapter.

(7) An assessment of budgetary savings resulting from this subchapter, including—

(A) a summary of the amount of savings resulting from the transfer of prisoners into prerelease custody under this chapter, including savings resulting from the avoidance or deferral of future construction, acquisition, or operations costs;

(B) a summary of the amount of savings resulting from any decrease in recidivism that may be attributed to the implementation of the risk and needs assessment system or the increase in recidivism reduction programs and productive activities required by this subchapter;

(C) a strategy to reinvest the savings described in subparagraphs (A) and (B) in other—

(i) Federal, State, and local law enforcement activities; and

(ii) expansions of recidivism reduction programs and productive activities in the Bureau of Prisons; and

(D) a description of how the reduced expenditures on Federal corrections and the budgetary savings resulting from this subchapter are currently being used and will be used to—

    (i) increase investment in law enforcement and crime prevention to combat gangs of national significance and high-level drug traffickers through the High Intensity Drug Trafficking Areas Program and other task forces;

    (ii) hire, train, and equip law enforcement officers and prosecutors; and

    (iii) promote crime reduction programs using evidence-based practices and strategic planning to help reduce crime and criminal recidivism.

(8) Statistics on—

    (A) the prevalence of dyslexia among prisoners in prisons operated by the Bureau of Prisons; and

    (B) any change in the effectiveness of dyslexia mitigation programs among such prisoners that may be attributed to the incorporation of dyslexia screening into the System and of dyslexia treatment into the evidence- based recidivism reduction programs, as required under this chapter.

Sec. 3635. Definitions

In this subchapter the following definitions apply:

(1) Dyslexia.—

The term "dyslexia" means an unexpected difficulty in reading for an individual who has the intelligence to be a much better reader, most commonly caused by a difficulty in the phonological processing (the appreciation of the individual sounds of spoken language), which affects the ability of an individual to speak, read, and spell.

(2) Dyslexia screening program.—

The term "dyslexia screening program" means a screening program for dyslexia that is—

(A) evidence-based (as defined in section 8101(21) of the Elementary and Secondary Education Act of 1965 (20 U.S.C. 7801(21) (https://www.law.cornell.edu/uscode/text/20/7801#21))) with proven psychometrics for validity;

(B) efficient and low-cost; and

(C) readily available.

(3) Evidence-based recidivism reduction program.—

The term "evidence-based recidivism reduction program" means either a group or individual activity that—

(A) has been shown by empirical evidence to reduce recidivism or is based on research indicating that it is likely to be effective in reducing recidivism;

(B) is designed to help prisoners succeed in their communities upon release from prison; and

(C) may include—

(i) social learning and communication, interpersonal, anti-bullying, rejection response, and other life skills;

(ii) family relationship building, structured parent-child interaction, and parenting skills;

(iii) classes on morals or ethics;

(iv) academic classes;

(v) cognitive behavioral treatment;

(vi) mentoring;

(vii) substance abuse treatment;

(viii) vocational training;

(ix) faith-based classes or services;

(x) civic engagement and reintegrative community services;

(xi) a prison job, including through a prison work program;

(xii) victim impact classes or other restorative justice programs; and

(xiii) trauma counseling and trauma-informed support programs.

(4) Prisoner.—

The term "prisoner" means a person who has been sentenced to a term of imprisonment pursuant to a conviction for a Federal criminal offense, or a person in the custody of the Bureau of Prisons.

(5) Productive activity.—

The term "productive activity" means either a group or individual activity that is designed to allow prisoners determined as having a minimum or low risk of recidivating to remain productive and thereby maintain a minimum or low risk of recidivating, and may include the delivery of the programs described in paragraph (1) to other prisoners.

(6) Risk and needs assessment tool.—

The term "risk and needs assessment tool" means an objective and statistically validated method through which information is collected and evaluated to determine—

(A) as part of the intake process, the risk that a prisoner will recidivate upon release from prison;

(B) the recidivism reduction programs that will best minimize the risk that the prisoner will recidivate upon release from prison; and

(C) the periodic reassessment of risk that a prisoner will recidivate upon release from prison, based on factors including indicators of progress and of regression, that are dynamic and that can reasonably be expected to change while in prison.

(b) Clerical amendment.—

The table of subchapters for chapter 229 of title 18, United States Code, is amended by adding at the end the following:

Sec. 102. Implementation of system and recommendations by Bureau of Prisons

(a) Implementation of system generally.—

Section 3621 of title 18 (https://www.law.cornell.edu/uscode/text/18/3621), United States Code, is amended by adding at the end the following:

(h) Implementation of risk and needs assessment system.—

(1) In general.—

Not later than 180 days after the Attorney General completes and releases the risk and needs assessment system (referred to in this subsection as the "System") developed under subchapter D, the Director of the Bureau of Prisons shall, in accordance with that subchapter—

(A) implement and complete the initial intake risk and needs assessment for each prisoner (including for each prisoner who was a prisoner prior to the effective date of this subsection), regardless of the prisoner's length of imposed term of imprisonment, and begin to assign prisoners to appropriate evidence-based recidivism reduction programs based on that determination;

(B) begin to expand the effective evidence-based recidivism reduction programs and productive activities it offers and add any new evidence- based recidivism reduction programs and productive activities necessary to effectively implement the System; and

(C) begin to implement the other risk and needs assessment tools necessary to effectively implement the System over time, while prisoners are participating in and completing the effective evidence- based recidivism reduction programs and productive activities.

(2) Phase-in.—

In order to carry out paragraph (1), so that every prisoner has the opportunity to participate in and complete the type and amount of evidence-based recidivism reduction programs or productive activities they need, and be reassessed for recidivism risk as necessary to effectively implement the System, the Bureau of Prisons shall—

(A) provide such evidence-based recidivism reduction programs and productive activities for all prisoners before the date that is 2 years after the date on which the Bureau of Prisons completes a risk and needs assessment for each prisoner under paragraph (1)(A); and

(B) develop and validate the risk and needs assessment tool to be used in the reassessments of risk of recidivism, while prisoners are participating in and completing evidence-based recidivism reduction programs and productive activities.

(3) Priority during phase-in.—
During the 2-year period described in paragraph (2)(A), the priority for such programs and activities shall be accorded based on a prisoner's proximity to release date.

(4) Preliminary expansion of evidence-based recidivism reduction programs and authority to use incentives.—

Beginning on the date of enactment of this subsection, the Bureau of Prisons may begin to expand any evidence-based recidivism reduction programs and productive activities that exist at a prison as of such date, and may offer to prisoners who successfully participate in such programs and activities the incentives and rewards described in subchapter D.

(5) Recidivism reduction partnerships.—

In order to expand evidence-based recidivism reduction programs and productive activities, the Attorney General shall develop policies for the warden of each prison of the Bureau of Prisons to enter into partnerships, subject to the availability of appropriations, with any of the following:

(A) Nonprofit and other private organizations, including faith-based, art, and community-based organizations that will deliver recidivism reduction programming on a paid or volunteer basis.

(B) Institutions of higher education (as defined in section 101 of the Higher Education Act of 1965 (20 U.S.C. 1001 (https://www.law.cornell.edu/uscode/text/20/1001))) that will deliver instruction on a paid or volunteer basis.

(C) Private entities that will—

    (i) deliver vocational training and certifications;

    (ii) provide equipment to facilitate vocational training or employment opportunities for prisoners;

    (iii) employ prisoners; or

    (iv) assist prisoners in prerelease custody or supervised release in finding employment.

(D) Industry-sponsored organizations that will deliver workforce development and training, on a paid or volunteer basis.

(6) Requirement to provide programs to all prisoners; priority.—

The Director of the Bureau of Prisons shall provide all prisoners with the opportunity to actively participate in evidence-based recidivism reduction programs or productive activities, according to their specific criminogenic needs, throughout their entire term of incarceration. Priority for participation in recidivism reduction programs shall be given to medium- risk and high-risk prisoners, with access to productive activities given to minimum-risk and low-risk prisoners.

(7) Definitions.—

The terms in this subsection have the meaning given those terms in section 3635.

(b) Prerelease custody.—

(1) In general.—

Section 3624 of title 18 (https://www.law.cornell.edu/uscode/text/18/3624), United States Code, is amended—

(A) in subsection (b)(1)—

(i) by striking ", beyond the time served, of up to 54 days at the end of each year of the prisoner's term of imprisonment, beginning at the end of the first year of the term," and inserting "of up to 54 days for each year of the prisoner's sentence imposed by the court,"; and

(ii) by striking "credit for the last year or portion of a year of the term of imprisonment shall be prorated and credited within the last six weeks of the sentence" and inserting "credit for the last year of a term of imprisonment shall be credited on the first day of the last year of the term of imprisonment"; and

(B) by adding at the end the following:

(g) Prerelease custody or supervised release for risk and needs assessment system participants.—

(1) Eligible prisoners.—

This subsection applies in the case of a prisoner (as such term is defined in section 3635) who—

(A) has earned time credits under the risk and needs assessment system developed under subchapter D (referred to in this subsection as the "System") in an amount that is equal to the remainder of the prisoner's imposed term of imprisonment;

(B) has shown through the periodic risk reassessments a demonstrated recidivism risk reduction or has maintained a minimum or low recidivism risk, during the prisoner's term of imprisonment;

(C) has had the remainder of the prisoner's imposed term of imprisonment computed under applicable law; and

(D)

   (i) in the case of a prisoner being placed in prerelease custody, the prisoner—

      (I) has been determined under the System to be a minimum or low risk to recidivate pursuant to the last 2 reassessments of the prisoner; or

      (II) has had a petition to be transferred to prerelease custody or supervised release approved by the warden of the prison, after the warden's determination that— (aa)the prisoner would not be a danger to society if transferred to prerelease custody or supervised release; (bb)the prisoner has made a good faith effort to lower their recidivism risk through participation in recidivism reduction programs or productive activities; and
      (cc)the prisoner is unlikely to recidivate; or

   (ii) in the case of a prisoner being placed in supervised release, the prisoner has been determined under the System to be a minimum or low risk to recidivate pursuant to the last reassessment of the prisoner.

(2) Types of prerelease custody.—

A prisoner shall be placed in prerelease custody as follows:

(A) Home confinement.—

   (i) In general.—

   A prisoner placed in prerelease custody pursuant to this subsection who is placed in home confinement shall—

   (I) be subject to 24-hour electronic monitoring that enables the prompt identification of the prisoner, location, and time, in the case of any violation of subclause (II);

   (II) remain in the prisoner's residence, except that the prisoner may leave the prisoner's home in order to, subject to the approval of the Director of the Bureau of Prisons—
   (aa) perform a job or job-related activities, including an apprenticeship, or participate in job-seeking activities;
   (bb) participate in evidence-based recidivism reduction programming or productive activities assigned by the System, or similar activities;
   (cc) perform community service;
   (dd) participate in crime victim restoration activities;
   (ee) receive medical treatment;
   (ff) attend religious activities; or
   (gg) participate in other family-related activities that facilitate the prisoner's successful reentry such as a family funeral, a family wedding, or to visit a family member who is seriously ill; and

   (III) comply with such other conditions as the Director determines appropriate.

   (ii) Alternate means of monitoring.—

   If the electronic monitoring of a prisoner described in clause (i)(I) is infeasible for technical or religious reasons, the Director of the Bureau of Prisons may use alternative means of monitoring a prisoner placed in home confinement that the Director determines are as effective or more effective than the electronic monitoring described in clause (i)(I).

      (iii) Modifications.—

The Director of the Bureau of Prisons may modify the conditions described in clause (i) if the Director determines that a compelling reason exists to do so, and that the prisoner has demonstrated exemplary compliance with such conditions.

      (iv) Duration.—

Except as provided in paragraph (4), a prisoner who is placed in home confinement shall remain in home confinement until the prisoner has served not less than 85 percent of the prisoner's imposed term of imprisonment.

   (B) Residential reentry center.—

A prisoner placed in prerelease custody pursuant to this subsection who is placed at a residential reentry center shall be subject to such conditions as the Director of the Bureau of Prisons determines appropriate.

(3) Supervised release.—

If the sentencing court included as a part of the prisoner's sentence a requirement that the prisoner be placed on a term of supervised release after imprisonment pursuant to section 3583, the Director of the Bureau of Prisons may transfer the prisoner to begin any such term of supervised release at an earlier date, not to exceed 12 months, based on the application of time credits under section 3632.

(4) Determination of conditions.—

In determining appropriate conditions for prisoners placed in prerelease custody pursuant to this subsection, the Director of the Bureau of Prisons shall, to the extent practicable, provide that increasingly less restrictive conditions shall be imposed on prisoners who demonstrate continued compliance with the conditions of such prerelease custody, so as to most effectively prepare such prisoners for reentry.

(5) Violations of conditions.—

If a prisoner violates a condition of the prisoner's prerelease custody, the Director of the Bureau of Prisons may impose such additional conditions on the prisoner's prerelease custody as the Director of the Bureau of Prisons determines appropriate, or revoke the prisoner's prerelease custody and require the prisoner to serve the remainder of the term of imprisonment to which the prisoner was sentenced, or any portion thereof, in prison. If the violation is nontechnical in nature, the Director of the Bureau of Prisons shall revoke the prisoner's prerelease custody.

(6) Issuance of guidelines.—

The Attorney General, in consultation with the Assistant Director for the Office of Probation and Pretrial Services, shall issue guidelines for use by the Bureau of Prisons in determining—

(A) the appropriate type of prerelease custody or supervised release and level of supervision for a prisoner placed on prerelease custody pursuant to this subsection; and

(B) consequences for a violation of a condition of such prerelease custody by such a prisoner, including a return to prison and a reassessment of evidence-based recidivism risk level under the System.

(7) Agreements with United States probation and pretrial services.—

The Director of the Bureau of Prisons shall, to the greatest extent practicable, enter into agreements with United States Probation and Pretrial Services to supervise prisoners placed in home confinement under this subsection. Such agreements shall—

(A) authorize United States Probation and Pretrial Services to exercise the authority granted to the Director pursuant to paragraphs (3) and (4); and

(B) take into account the resource requirements of United States Probation and Pretrial Services as a result of the transfer of Bureau of Prisons prisoners to prerelease custody or supervised release.

(8) Assistance.—

United States Probation and Pretrial Services shall, to the greatest extent practicable, offer assistance to any prisoner not under its supervision during prerelease custody under this subsection.

(9) Mentoring, reentry, and spiritual services.—

Any prerelease custody into which a prisoner is placed under this subsection may not include a condition prohibiting the prisoner from receiving mentoring, reentry, or spiritual services from a person who provided such services to the prisoner while the prisoner was incarcerated, except that the warden of the facility at which the prisoner was incarcerated may waive the requirement under this paragraph if the warden finds that the provision of such services would pose a significant security risk to the prisoner, persons who provide such services, or any other person. The warden shall provide written notice of any such waiver to the person providing such services and to the prisoner.

(10) Time limits inapplicable.—

The time limits under subsections (b) and (c) shall not apply to prerelease custody under this subsection.

(11) Prerelease custody capacity.—

The Director of the Bureau of Prisons shall ensure there is sufficient prerelease custody capacity to accommodate all eligible prisoners.

(2) Effective date.—

The amendments made by this subsection shall take effect beginning on the date that the Attorney General completes and releases the risk and needs assessment system under subchapter D of chapter 229 of title 18, United States Code, as added by section 101(a) of this Act.

(3) Applicability.—

The amendments made by this subsection shall apply with respect to offenses committed before, on, or after the date of enactment of this Act, except that such amendments shall not apply with respect to offenses committed before November 1, 1987.

Sec. 103. GAO report

Not later than 2 years after the Director of the Bureau of Prisons implements the risk and needs assessment system under section 3621 of title 18 (https://www.law.cornell.edu/uscode/text/18/3621), United States Code, and every 2 years thereafter, the Comptroller General of the United States shall conduct an audit of the use of the risk and needs assessment system at Bureau of Prisons facilities. The audit shall include analysis of the following:

(1) Whether inmates are being assessed under the risk and needs assessment system with the frequency required under such section 3621 of title 18 (https://www.law.cornell.edu/uscode/text/18/3621), United States Code.

(2) Whether the Bureau of Prisons is able to offer recidivism reduction programs and productive activities (as such terms are defined in section 3635 of title 18 (https://www.law.cornell.edu/uscode/text/18/3635), United States Code, as added by section 101(a) of this Act).

(3) Whether the Bureau of Prisons is offering the type, amount, and intensity of recidivism reduction programs and productive activities for prisoners to earn the maximum amount of time credits for which they are eligible.

(4) Whether the Attorney General is carrying out the duties under section 3631(b) of title 18 (https://www.law.cornell.edu/uscode/text/18/3631#b), United States Code, as added by section 101(a) of this Act.

(5) Whether officers and employees of the Bureau of Prisons are receiving the training described in section 3632(f) of title 18 (https://www.law.cornell.edu/uscode/text/18/3632#f), United States Code, as added by section 101(a) of this Act.

(6) Whether the Bureau of Prisons offers work assignments to all prisoners who might benefit from such an assignment.

(7) Whether the Bureau of Prisons transfers prisoners to prerelease custody or supervised release as soon as they are eligible for such a transfer under section 3624(g) of title 18 (https://www.law.cornell.edu/uscode/text/18/3624#g), United States Code, as added by section 102(b) of this Act.

(8) The rates of recidivism among similarly classified prisoners to identify any unwarranted disparities, including disparities among similarly classified prisoners of different demographic groups, in such rates.

Sec. 104. Authorization of appropriations

(a) In general.—

There is authorized to be appropriated to carry out this title $75,000,000 for each of fiscal years 2019 through 2023. Of the amount appropriated under this subsection, 80 percent shall be reserved for use by the Director of the Bureau of Prisons to implement the system under section 3621(h) of title 18 (https://www.law.cornell.edu/uscode/text/18/3621#h), United States Code, as added by section 102(a) of this Act.

(b) Savings.—

It is the sense of Congress that any savings associated with reductions in recidivism that result from this title should be reinvested—

(1) to supplement funding for programs that increase public safety by providing resources to State and local law enforcement officials, including for the adoption of innovative technologies and information sharing capabilities;

(2) into evidence-based recidivism reduction programs offered by the Bureau of Prisons; and

(3) into ensuring eligible prisoners have access to such programs and productive activities offered by the Bureau of Prisons.

Sec. 105. Rule of construction

Nothing in this Act, or the amendments made by this Act, may be construed to provide authority to place a prisoner in prerelease custody or supervised release who is serving a term of imprisonment pursuant to a conviction for an offense under the laws of one of the 50 States, or of a territory or possession of the United States or to amend or affect the enforcement of the immigration laws, as defined in section 101 of the Immigration and Nationality Act (8 U.S.C. 1101 (https://www.law.cornell.edu/uscode/text/8/1101)).

Sec. 106. Faith-based considerations

(a) In general.—

In considering any program, treatment, regimen, group, company, charity, person, or entity of any kind under any provision of this Act, or the amendments made by this Act, the fact that it may be or is faith-based may not be a basis for any discrimination against it in any manner or for any purpose.

(b) Eligibility for earned time credit.—

Participation in a faith-based program, treatment, or regimen may qualify a prisoner for earned time credit under subchapter D of chapter 229 of title 18, United States Code, as added by section 101(a) of this Act, however, the Director of the Bureau of Prisons shall ensure that non-faith-based programs that qualify for earned time credit are offered at each Bureau of Prisons facility in addition to any such faith-based programs.

(c) Limitation on activities.—

A group, company, charity, person, or entity may not engage in explicitly religious activities using direct financial assistance made available under this title or the amendments made by this title.

(d) Rule of construction.—

Nothing in this Act, or the amendments made by this Act, may be construed to amend any requirement under Federal law or the Constitution of the United States regarding funding for faith-based programs or activities.

Sec. 107. Independent Review Committee

(a) In general.—

The Attorney General shall consult with an Independent Review Committee in carrying out the Attorney General's duties under sections 3631(b), 3632 and 3633 of title 18, United States Code, as added by section 101(a) of this Act.

(b) Formation of Independent Review Committee.—

The National Institute of Justice shall select a nonpartisan and nonprofit organization with expertise in the study and development of risk and needs assessment tools to host the Independent Review Committee. The Independent Review Committee shall be established not later than 30 days after the date of enactment of this Act.

(c) Appointment of Independent Review Committee.—

The organization selected by the National Institute of Justice shall appoint not fewer than 6 members to the Independent Review Committee.

(d) Composition of the Independent Review Committee.—

The members of the Independent Review Committee shall all have expertise in risk and needs assessment systems and shall include—

(1) 2 individuals who have published peer-reviewed scholarship about risk and needs assessments in both corrections and community settings;

(2) 2 corrections practitioners who have developed and implemented a risk assessment tool in a corrections system or in a community supervision setting, including 1 with prior experience working within the Bureau of Prisons; and

(3) 1 individual with expertise in assessing risk assessment implementation.

(e) Duties of the Independent Review Committee.—

The Independent Review Committee shall assist the Attorney General in carrying out the Attorney General's duties under sections 3631(b), 3632 and 3633 of title 18, United States Code, as added by section 101(a) of this Act, including by assisting in—

(1) conducting a review of the existing prisoner risk and needs assessment systems in operation on the date of enactment of this Act;

(2) developing recommendations regarding evidence-based recidivism reduction programs and productive activities;

(3) conducting research and data analysis on—

(A) evidence-based recidivism reduction programs relating to the use of prisoner risk and needs assessment tools;

(B) the most effective and efficient uses of such programs; and

(C) which evidence-based recidivism reduction programs are the most effective at reducing recidivism, and the type, amount, and intensity of programming that most effectively reduces the risk of recidivism; and

(4) reviewing and validating the risk and needs assessment system.

(f) Bureau of Prisons cooperation.—

The Director of the Bureau of Prisons shall assist the Independent Review Committee in performing the Committee's duties and promptly respond to requests from the Committee for access to Bureau of Prisons facilities, personnel, and information.

(g) Report.—

Not later than 2 years after the date of enactment of this Act, the Independent Review Committee shall submit to the Committee on the Judiciary and the Subcommittee on Commerce, Justice, Science, and Related Agencies of the Committee on Appropriations of the Senate and the Committee on the Judiciary and the Subcommittee on Commerce, Justice, Science, and Related Agencies of the Committee on Appropriations of the House of Representatives a report that includes—

(1) a list of all offenses of conviction for which prisoners were ineligible to receive time credits under section 3632(d)(4)(D) of title 18 (https://www.law.cornell.edu/uscode/text/18/3632#d_4_D), United States Code, as added by section 101(a) of this Act, and for each offense the number of prisoners excluded, including demographic percentages by age, race, and sex;

(2) the criminal history categories of prisoners ineligible to receive time credits under section 3632(d)(4)(D) of title 18 (https://www.law.cornell.edu/uscode/text/18/3632#d_4_D), United States Code, as added by section 101(a) of this Act, and for each category the number of prisoners excluded, including demographic percentages by age, race, and sex;

(3) the number of prisoners ineligible to apply time credits under section 3632(d)(4)(D) of title 18 (https://www.law.cornell.edu/uscode/text/18/3632#d_4_D), United States Code, as added by section 101(a) of this Act, who do not participate in recidivism reduction programming or productive activities, including the demographic percentages by age, race, and sex;

(4) any recommendations for modifications to section 3632(d)(4)(D) of title 18 (https://www.law.cornell.edu/uscode/text/18/3632#d_4_D), United States Code, as added by section 101(a) of this Act, and any other recommendations regarding recidivism reduction.

(h) Termination.—

The Independent Review Committee shall terminate on the date that is 2 years after the date on which the risk and needs assessment system authorized by sections 3632 and 3633 of title 18, United States Code, as added by section 101(a) of this Act, is released.

Title II

Bureau of Prisons secure firearms storage

Sec. 201. Short title

This title may be cited as the "Lieutenant Osvaldo Albarati Correctional Officer Self-Protection Act of 2018".

Sec. 202. Secure firearms storage

(a) In general.— Chapter 303 of title 18, United States Code, is amended by adding at the end the following:

Sec. 4050. Secure firearms storage

(a) Definitions.—

In this section—

(1) the term "employee" means a qualified law enforcement officer employed by the Bureau of Prisons; and

(2) the terms "firearm" and "qualified law enforcement officer" have the meanings given those terms under section 926B.

(b) Secure firearms storage.—

The Director of the Bureau of Prisons shall ensure that each chief executive officer of a Federal penal or correctional institution—

(1)

(A) provides a secure storage area located outside of the secure perimeter of the institution for employees to store firearms; or

(B) allows employees to store firearms in a vehicle lockbox approved by the Director of the Bureau of Prisons; and

(2) notwithstanding any other provision of law, allows employees to carry concealed firearms on the premises outside of the secure perimeter of the institution.

(b) Technical and conforming amendment.—

The table of sections for chapter 303 of title 18, United States Code, is amended by adding at the end the following:

4050. Secure firearms storage.

Title III
Restraints on pregnant prisoners prohibited

Sec. 301. Use of restraints on prisoners during the period of pregnancy and postpartum recovery prohibited

(a) In general.—

Chapter 317 of title 18, United States Code, is amended by inserting after section 4321 the following:

Sec. 4322. Use of restraints on prisoners during the period of pregnancy, labor, and postpartum recovery prohibited

(a) Prohibition.—

Except as provided in subsection (b), beginning on the date on which pregnancy is confirmed by a healthcare professional, and ending at the conclusion of postpartum recovery, a prisoner in the custody of the Bureau of Prisons, or in the custody of the United States Marshals Service pursuant to section 4086, shall not be placed in restraints.

(b) Exceptions.—

(1) In general.—

The prohibition under subsection (a) shall not apply if—

(A) an appropriate corrections official, or a United States marshal, as applicable, makes a determination that the prisoner—

(i) is an immediate and credible flight risk that cannot reasonably be prevented by other means; or

(ii) poses an immediate and serious threat of harm to herself or others that cannot reasonably be prevented by other means; or

(B) a healthcare professional responsible for the health and safety of the prisoner determines that the use of restraints is appropriate for the medical safety of the prisoner.

(2) Least restrictive restraints.—

In the case that restraints are used pursuant to an exception under paragraph (1), only the least restrictive restraints necessary to prevent the harm or risk of escape described in paragraph (1) may be used.

(3) Application.—

(A) In general.—

The exceptions under paragraph (1) may not be applied—

(i) to place restraints around the ankles, legs, or waist of a prisoner;

(ii) to restrain a prisoner's hands behind her back;

(iii) to restrain a prisoner using 4-point restraints; or

(iv) to attach a prisoner to another prisoner.

(B) Medical request.—

Notwithstanding paragraph (1), upon the request of a healthcare professional who is responsible for the health and safety of a prisoner, a corrections official or United States marshal, as applicable, shall refrain from using restraints on the prisoner or shall remove restraints used on the prisoner.

(c) Reports.—

(1) Report to the Director and healthcare professional.—

If a corrections official or United States marshal uses restraints on a prisoner under subsection (b)(1), that official or marshal shall submit, not later than 30 days after placing the prisoner in restraints, to the Director of the Bureau of Prisons or the Director of the United States Marshals Service, as applicable, and to the healthcare professional responsible for the health and safety of the prisoner, a written report that describes the facts and circumstances surrounding the use of restraints, and includes—

(A) the reasoning upon which the determination to use restraints was made;

(B) the details of the use of restraints, including the type of restraints used and length of time during which restraints were used; and

(C) any resulting physical effects on the prisoner observed by or known to the corrections official or United States marshal, as applicable.

(2) Supplemental report to the director.—

Upon receipt of a report under paragraph (1), the healthcare professional responsible for the health and safety of the prisoner may submit to the Director such information as the healthcare professional determines is relevant to the use of restraints on the prisoner.

(3) Report to Judiciary committees.—

(A) In general.—

Not later than 1 year after the date of enactment of this section, and annually thereafter, the Director of the Bureau of Prisons and the Director of the United States Marshals Service shall each submit to the Judiciary Committee of the Senate and of the House of Representatives a report that certifies compliance with this section and includes the information required to be reported under paragraph (1).

(B) Personally identifiable information.—

The report under this paragraph shall not contain any personally identifiable information of any prisoner.

(d) Notice.—

Not later than 48 hours after the confirmation of a prisoner's pregnancy by a healthcare professional, that prisoner shall be notified by an appropriate healthcare professional, corrections official, or United States marshal, as applicable, of the restrictions on the use of restraints under this section.

(e) Violation reporting process.—

The Director of the Bureau of Prisons, in consultation with the Director of the United States Marshals Service, shall establish a process through which a prisoner may report a violation of this section.

(f) Training.—

(1) In general.—

The Director of the Bureau of Prisons and the Director of the United States Marshals Service shall each develop training guidelines regarding the use of restraints on female prisoners during the period of pregnancy, labor, and postpartum recovery, and shall incorporate such guidelines into appropriate training programs. Such training guidelines shall include—

(A) how to identify certain symptoms of pregnancy that require immediate referral to a healthcare professional;

(B) circumstances under which the exceptions under subsection (b) would apply;

(C) in the case that an exception under subsection (b) applies, how to apply restraints in a way that does not harm the prisoner, the fetus, or the neonate;

(D) the information required to be reported under subsection (c); and

(E) the right of a healthcare professional to request that restraints not be used, and the requirement under subsection (b)(3)(B) to comply with such a request.

(2) Development of guidelines.—

In developing the guidelines required by paragraph (1), the Directors shall each consult with healthcare professionals with expertise in caring for women during the period of pregnancy and postpartum recovery.

(g) Definitions.—

For purposes of this section:

(1) Postpartum recovery.—

The term "postpartum recovery" means the 12-week period, or longer as determined by the healthcare professional responsible for the health and safety of the prisoner, following delivery, and shall include the entire period that the prisoner is in the hospital or infirmary.

(2) Prisoner.—

The term "prisoner" means a person who has been sentenced to a term of imprisonment pursuant to a conviction for a Federal criminal offense, or a person in the custody of the Bureau of Prisons, including a person in a Bureau of Prisons contracted facility.

(3) Restraints.—

The term "restraints" means **any** physical or mechanical device used to control the movement of a prisoner's body, limbs, or both.

(b) Clerical amendment.—

The table of sections for chapter 317 of title 18, United States Code, is amended by adding after the item relating to section 4321 the following:

4322. Use of restraints on prisoners during the period of pregnancy, labor, and postpartum recovery prohibited.

Title IV

Sentencing reform

Sec. 401. Reduce and restrict enhanced sentencing for prior drug felonies

(a) Controlled Substances Act amendments.—

The Controlled Substances Act (21 U.S.C. 801 (https://www.law.cornell.edu/uscode/text/21/801) et seq.) is amended—

(1) in section 102 (21 U.S.C. 802 (https://www.law.cornell.edu/uscode/text/21/802)), by adding at the end the following:

(57) The term "serious drug felony" means an offense described in section 924 (e)(2) of title 18 (https://www.law.cornell.edu/uscode/text/18/924#e_2), United States Code, for which—

   (A) the offender served a term of imprisonment of more than 12 months; and

   (B) the offender's release from any term of imprisonment was within 15 years of the commencement of the instant offense.

(58) The term "serious violent felony" means—
   (A) an offense described in section 3559(c)(2) of title 18 (https://www.law.cornell.edu/uscode/text/18/3559#c_2), United States Code, for which the offender served a term of imprisonment of more than 12 months; and

   (B) any offense that would be a felony violation of section 113 of title 18 (https://www.law.cornell.edu/uscode/text/18/113), United States Code, if the offense were committed in the special maritime and territorial jurisdiction of the United States, for which the offender served a term of imprisonment of more than 12 months; and

(2) in section 401(b)(1) (21 U.S.C. 841(b)(1) (https://www.law.cornell.edu/uscode/text/21/841#b_1))—

   (A) in subparagraph (A), in the matter following clause (viii)—

      (i) by striking "If any person commits such a violation after a prior conviction for a felony drug offense has become final, such person shall be sentenced to a term of imprisonment which may not be less than 20 years" and inserting the following: "If any person commits such a violation after a prior conviction for a serious drug felony or serious violent felony has become final, such person shall be sentenced to a term of imprisonment of not less than 15 years"; and

      (ii) by striking "after two or more prior convictions for a felony drug offense have become final, such person shall be sentenced to a mandatory term of life imprisonment without release" and inserting the following: "after 2 or more prior convictions for a serious drug felony or serious violent felony have become final, such person shall be sentenced to a term of imprisonment of not less than 25 years"; and

(B) in subparagraph (B), in the matter following clause (viii), by striking "If any person commits such a violation after a prior conviction for a felony drug offense has become final" and inserting the following: "If any person commits such a violation after a prior conviction for a serious drug felony or serious violent felony has become final".

(b) Controlled Substances Import and Export Act amendments.—

Section 1010(b) of the Controlled Substances Import and Export Act (21 U.S.C. 960(b) (https://www.law.cornell.edu/uscode/text/21/960#b)) is amended—

(1) in paragraph (1), in the matter following subparagraph (H), by striking "If any person commits such a violation after a prior conviction for a felony drug offense has become final, such person shall be sentenced to a term of imprisonment of not less than 20 years" and inserting "If any person commits such a violation after a prior conviction for a serious drug felony or serious violent felony has become final, such person shall be sentenced to a term of imprisonment of not less than 15 years"; and

(2) in paragraph (2), in the matter following subparagraph (H), by striking "felony drug offense" and inserting "serious drug felony or serious violent felony".

(c) Applicability to pending cases.—
This section, and the amendments made by this section, shall apply to any offense that was committed before the date of enactment of this Act, if a sentence for the offense has not been imposed as of such date of enactment.

Sec. 402. Broadening of existing safety valve

(a) Amendments.—

Section 3553 of title 18 (https://www.law.cornell.edu/uscode/text/18/3553), United States Code, is amended—

(1) in subsection (f)—

(A) in the matter preceding paragraph (1)—

(i) by striking "or section 1010" and inserting ", section 1010"; and

(ii) by inserting ", or section 70503 or 70506 of title 46" after "963)";

(1) the defendant does not have—

    (A) more than 4 criminal history points, excluding any criminal history points resulting from a 1-point offense, as determined under the sentencing guidelines;

    (B) a prior 3-point offense, as determined under the sentencing guidelines; and

(B) by striking paragraph (1) and inserting the following:

> > (C) a **prior** 2-point violent offense, as determined under the sentencing guidelines; and

> (C) by adding at the end the following:

> > Information disclosed by a defendant under this subsection may not be used to enhance the sentence of the defendant unless the information relates to a violent offense; and

> (2) by adding at the end the following:

> > (g) Definition of violent offense.—

> > > As used in this section, the term "violent offense" means a crime of violence, as defined in section 16, that is punishable by imprisonment.

(b) Applicability.—

The amendments made by this section shall apply only to a conviction entered on or after the date of enactment of this Act.

Sec. 403. Clarification of section 924(c) of title 18, United States Code

(a) In general.—

Section 924(c)(1)(C) of title 18 (https://www.law.cornell.edu/uscode/text/18/924#c_1_C), United States Code, is amended, in the matter preceding clause (i), by striking "second or subsequent conviction under this subsection" and inserting "violation of this subsection that occurs after a prior conviction under this subsection has become final".

(b) Applicability to pending cases.—

This section, and the amendments made by this section, shall apply to any offense that was committed before the date of enactment of this Act, if a sentence for the offense has not been imposed as of such date of enactment.

Sec. 404. Application of Fair Sentencing Act

(a) Definition of covered offense.—

In this section, the term "covered offense" means a violation of a Federal criminal statute, the statutory penalties for which were modified by section 2 or 3 of the Fair Sentencing Act of 2010 (Public Law 111–220 (https://www.govtrack.us/search? q=PubLaw+111-220); 124 Stat. 2372 (http://api.fdsys.gov/link? collection=statute&volume=124&page=2372)), that was committed before August 3, 2010.

(b) Defendants previously sentenced.—

A court that imposed a sentence for a covered offense may, on motion of the defendant, the Director of the Bureau of Prisons, the attorney for the Government, or the court, impose a reduced sentence as if sections 2 and 3 of the Fair Sentencing Act of 2010 (Public Law 111–220 (https://www.govtrack.us/search?q=PubLaw+111-220); 124 Stat. 2372 (http://api.fdsys.gov/link?collection=statute&volume=124&page=2372)) were in effect at the time the covered offense was committed.

(c) Limitations.—

No court shall entertain a motion made under this section to reduce a sentence if the sentence was previously imposed or previously reduced in accordance with the amendments made by sections 2 and 3 of the Fair Sentencing Act of 2010 (Public Law 111–220 (https://www.govtrack.us/search?q=PubLaw+111-220); 124 Stat. 2372 (http://api.fdsys.gov/link?collection=statute&volume=124&page=2372)) or if a previous motion made under this section to reduce the sentence was, after the date of enactment of this Act, denied after a complete review of the motion on the merits. Nothing in this section shall be construed to require a court to reduce any sentence pursuant to this section.

Title V

Second Chance Act of 2007 reauthorization

Sec. 501. Short title

This title may be cited as the "Second Chance Reauthorization Act of 2018".

Sec. 502. Improvements to existing programs

(a) Reauthorization of adult and juvenile offender State and local demonstration projects.

Section 2976 of title I of the Omnibus Crime Control and Safe Streets Act of 1968 (34 U.S.C. 10631 (https://www.law.cornell.edu/uscode/text/34/10631)) is amended—

(1) by striking subsection (a) and inserting the following:

(a) Grant authorization.—

The Attorney General shall make grants to States, local governments, territories, or Indian tribes, or any combination thereof (in this section referred to as an "eligible entity"), in partnership with interested persons (including Federal corrections and supervision agencies), service providers, and nonprofit organizations for the purpose of strategic planning and implementation of adult and juvenile offender reentry projects;

(2) in subsection (b)—

(A) in paragraph (3), by inserting "or reentry courts," after "community,";

(B) in paragraph (6), by striking "and" at the end;

(C) in paragraph (7), by striking the period at the end and inserting "; and"; and

(D) by adding at the end the following:

(8) promoting employment opportunities consistent with the Transitional Jobs strategy (as defined in section 4 of the Second Chance Act of 2007 (34 U.S.C. 60502 (https://www.law.cornell.edu/uscode/text/34/60502))); and

(3) by striking subsections (d), (e), and (f) and inserting the following:

(d) Combined grant application; priority consideration.—

(1) In general.—

The Attorney General shall develop a procedure to allow applicants to submit a single application for a planning grant under subsection (e) and an implementation grant under subsection (f).

(2) Priority consideration.—

The Attorney General shall give priority consideration to grant applications under subsections (e) and (f) that include a commitment by the applicant to partner with a local evaluator to identify and analyze data that will—

(A) enable the grantee to target the intended offender population; and

(B) serve as a baseline for purposes of the evaluation.

(e) Planning grants.—

(1) In general.—

Except as provided in paragraph (3), the Attorney General may make a grant to an eligible entity of not more than $75,000 to develop a strategic, collaborative plan for an adult or juvenile offender reentry demonstration project as described in subsection (h) that includes—

(A) a budget and a budget justification;

(B) a description of the outcome measures that will be used to measure the effectiveness of the program in promoting public safety and public health;

(C) the activities proposed;

(D) a schedule for completion of the activities described in subparagraph (C); and

(E) a description of the personnel necessary to complete the activities described in subparagraph(C).

(2) Maximum total grants and geographic diversity.—

(A) Maximum amount.—

The Attorney General may not make initial planning grants and implementation grants to 1 eligible entity in a total amount that is more than a $1,000,000.

(B) Geographic diversity.—

The Attorney General shall make every effort to ensure equitable geographic distribution of grants under this section and take into consideration the needs of underserved populations, including rural and tribal communities.

(3) Period of grant.—

A planning grant made under this subsection shall be for a period of not longer than 1 year, beginning on the first day of the month in which the planning grant is made.

(f) Implementation grants.—

(1) Applications.—

An eligible entity desiring an implementation grant under this subsection shall submit to the Attorney General an application that—

(A) contains a reentry strategic plan as described in subsection (h), which describes the long-term strategy and incorporates a detailed implementation schedule, including the plans of the applicant to fund the program after Federal funding is discontinued;

(B) identifies the local government role and the role of governmental agencies and nonprofit organizations that will be coordinated by, and that will collaborate on, the offender reentry strategy of the applicant, and certifies the involvement of such agencies and organizations;

(C) describes the evidence-based methodology and outcome measures that will be used to evaluate the program funded with a grant under this subsection, and specifically explains how such measurements will provide valid measures of the impact of that program; and

(D) describes how the project could be broadly replicated if demonstrated to be effective.

(2) Requirements.—

The Attorney General may make a grant to an applicant under this subsection only if the application—

(A) reflects explicit support of the chief executive officer, or their designee, of the State, unit of local government, territory, or Indian tribe applying for a grant under this subsection;

(B) provides discussion of the role of Federal corrections, State corrections departments, community corrections agencies, juvenile justice systems, and tribal or local jail systems in ensuring successful reentry of offenders into their communities;

(C) provides evidence of collaboration with State, local, or tribal government agencies overseeing health, housing, child welfare, education, substance abuse, victims services, and employment services, and with local law enforcement agencies;

(D) provides a plan for analysis of the statutory, regulatory, rules-based, and practice-based hurdles to reintegration of offenders into the community;

(E) includes the use of a State, local, territorial, or tribal task force, described in subsection (i), to carry out the activities funded under the grant;

(F) provides a plan for continued collaboration with a local evaluator as necessary to meeting the requirements under subsection (h); and

(G) demonstrates that the applicant participated in the planning grant process or engaged in comparable planning for the reentry project.

(3) Priority considerations.—

The Attorney General shall give priority to grant applications under this subsection that best—

(A) focus initiative on geographic areas with a disproportionate population of offenders released from prisons, jails, and juvenile facilities;

(B) include—

(i) input from nonprofit organizations, in any case where relevant input is available and appropriate to the grant application;

(ii) consultation with crime victims and offenders who are released from prisons, jails, and juvenile facilities;

(iii) coordination with families of offenders;

(iv) input, where appropriate, from the juvenile justice coordinating council of the region;

(v) input, where appropriate, from the reentry coordinating council of the region; or

(vi) input, where appropriate, from other interested persons;

(C) demonstrate effective case assessment and management abilities in order to provide comprehensive and continuous reentry, including—

(i) planning for prerelease transitional housing and community release that begins upon admission for juveniles and jail inmates, and, as appropriate, for prison inmates, depending on the length of the sentence;

(ii) establishing prerelease planning procedures to ensure that the eligibility of an offender for Federal, tribal, or State benefits upon release is established prior to release, subject to any limitations in law, and to ensure that offenders obtain all necessary referrals for reentry services, including assistance identifying and securing suitable housing; or

(iii) delivery of continuous and appropriate mental health services, drug treatment, medical care, job training and placement, educational services, vocational services, and any other service or support needed for reentry;

(D) review the process by which the applicant adjudicates violations of parole, probation, or supervision following release from prison, jail, or a juvenile facility, taking into account public safety and the use of graduated, community-based sanctions for minor and technical violations of parole, probation, or supervision (specifically those violations that are not otherwise, and independently, a violation of law);

(E) provide for an independent evaluation of reentry programs that include, to the maximum extent possible, random assignment and controlled studies to determine the effectiveness of such programs;

(F) target moderate and high-risk offenders for reentry programs through validated assessment tools; or

(G) target offenders with histories of homelessness, substance abuse, or mental illness, including a prerelease assessment of the housing status of the offender and behavioral health needs of the offender with clear coordination with mental health, substance abuse, and homelessness services systems to achieve stable and permanent housing outcomes with appropriate support service.

(4) Period of grant.—

A grant made under this subsection shall be effective for a 2-year period—

(A) beginning on the date on which the planning grant awarded under subsection (e) concludes; or

(B) in the case of an implementation grant awarded to an eligible entity that did not receive a planning grant, beginning on the date on which the implementation grant is awarded;

(4) in subsection (h)—

(A) by redesignating paragraphs (2) and (3) as paragraphs (3) and (4), respectively; and

(B) by striking paragraph (1) and inserting the following:

- -

(1) In general.—

As a condition of receiving financial assistance under subsection (f), each application shall develop a comprehensive reentry strategic plan that—

(A) contains a plan to assess inmate reentry needs and measurable annual and 3-year performance outcomes;

(B) uses, to the maximum extent possible, randomly assigned and controlled studies, or rigorous quasi-experimental studies with matched comparison groups, to determine the effectiveness of the program funded with a grant under subsection (f); and

(C) includes as a goal of the plan to reduce the rate of recidivism for offenders released from prison, jail or a juvenile facility with funds made available under subsection (f).

(2) Local evaluator.—

A partnership with a local evaluator described in subsection (d)(2) shall require the local evaluator to use the baseline data and target population characteristics developed under a subsection (e) planning grant to derive a target goal for recidivism reduction during the 3-year period beginning on the date of implementation of the program;

(5) in subsection (i)(1)—

(A) in the matter preceding subparagraph (A), by striking "under this section" and inserting "under subsection (f)"; and

(B) in subparagraph (B), by striking "subsection (e)(4)" and inserting "subsection (f)(2)(D)";

(6) in subsection (j)—

(A) in paragraph (1), by inserting "for an implementation grant under subsection (f)" after "applicant";

(B) in paragraph (2)—

(i) in subparagraph (E), by inserting ", where appropriate" after "support"; and

(ii) by striking subparagraphs (F), (G), and (H), and inserting the following:

(F) increased number of staff trained to administer reentry services;

(G) increased proportion of individuals served by the program among those eligible to receive services;

(H) increased number of individuals receiving risk screening needs assessment, and case planning services;

(I) increased enrollment in, and completion of treatment services, including substance abuse and mental health services among those assessed as needing such services;

(J) increased enrollment in and degrees earned from educational programs, including high school, GED, vocational training, and college education;

(K) increased number of individuals obtaining and retaining employment;

(L) increased number of individuals obtaining and maintaining housing;

(M) increased self-reports of successful community living, including stability of living situation and positive family relationships;

(N) reduction in drug and alcohol use; and

(O) reduction in recidivism rates for individuals receiving reentry services after release, as compared to either baseline recidivism rates in the jurisdiction of the grantee or recidivism rates of the control or comparison group;

(C) in paragraph (3), by striking "facilities." and inserting "facilities, including a cost-benefit analysis to determine the cost effectiveness of the reentry program.";

(D) in paragraph (4), by striking "this section" and inserting "subsection (f)"; and

(E) in paragraph (5), by striking "this section" and inserting "subsection (f)";

(7) in subsection (k)(1), by striking "this section" each place the term appears and inserting "subsection (f)";

(8) in subsection (l)—

(A) in paragraph (2), by inserting "beginning on the date on which the most recent implementation grant is made to the grantee under subsection (f)" after "2-year period"; and

(B) in paragraph (4), by striking "over a 2-year period" and inserting "during the 2-year period described in paragraph (2)";

(9) in subsection (o)(1), by striking "appropriated" and all that follows and inserting the following: "appropriated $35,000,000 for each of fiscal years 2019 through 2023."; and

(10) by adding at the end the following:

(p) Definition.—

In this section, the term "reentry court" means a program that—

(1) monitors juvenile and adult eligible offenders reentering the community;

(2) provides continual judicial supervision;

(3) provides juvenile and adult eligible offenders reentering the community with coordinated and comprehensive reentry services and programs, such as—

(A) drug and alcohol testing and assessment for treatment;

(B) assessment for substance abuse from a substance abuse professional who is approved by the State or Indian tribe and licensed by the appropriate entity to provide alcohol and drug addiction treatment, as appropriate;

(C) substance abuse treatment, including medication-assisted treatment, from a provider that is approved by the State or Indian tribe, and licensed, if necessary, to provide medical and other health services;

(D) health (including mental health) services and assessment;

(E) aftercare and case management services that—

(i) facilitate access to clinical care and related health services; and

(ii) coordinate with such clinical care and related health services; and

(F) any other services needed for reentry;

(4) convenes community impact panels, victim impact panels, or victim impact educational classes;

(5) provides and coordinates the delivery of community services to juvenile and adult eligible offenders, including—

(A) housing assistance;

(B) education;

(C) job training;

(D) conflict resolution skills training;

(E) batterer intervention programs; and

(F) other appropriate social services; and

(6) establishes and implements graduated sanctions and incentives.

(b) Grants for family-Based substance abuse treatment.—

Part DD of title I of the Omnibus Crime Control and Safe Streets Act of 1968 (34 U.S.C. 10591 (https://www.law.cornell.edu/uscode/text/34/10591) et seq.) is amended—

(1) in section 2921 (34 U.S.C. 10591 (https://www.law.cornell.edu/uscode/text/34/10591)), in the matter preceding paragraph (1), by inserting "nonprofit organizations," before "and Indian";

(2) in section 2923 (34 U.S.C. 10593 (https://www.law.cornell.edu/uscode/text/34/10593)), by adding at the end the following:

(c) Priority considerations.—

The Attorney General shall give priority consideration to grant applications for grants under section 2921 that are submitted by a nonprofit organization that demonstrates a relationship with State and local criminal justice agencies, including—

(1) within the judiciary and prosecutorial agencies; or

(2) with the local corrections agencies, which shall be documented by a written agreement that details the terms of access to facilities and participants and provides information on the history of the organization of working with correctional populations; and

(3) by striking section 2926(a) and inserting the following:

(a) In general

There are authorized to be appropriated to carry out this part $10,000,000 for each of fiscal years 2019 through 2023.

(c) Grant program To evaluate and improve educational methods at prisons, jails, and juvenile facilities.—

Title I of the Omnibus Crime Control and Safe Streets Act of 1968 (42 U.S.C. 3711 (https://www.law.cornell.edu/uscode/text/42/3711) et seq.) is amended—

(1) by striking the second part designated as part JJ, as added by the Second Chance Act of 2007 (Public Law 110–199 (https://www.govtrack.us/search?q=PubLaw+110-199); 122 Stat. 677 (http://api.fdsys.gov/link?collection=statute&volume=122&page=677)), relating to grants to evaluate and improve educational methods at prisons, jails, and juvenile facilities;

(2) by adding at the end the following:

Part NN

Grant program to evaluate and improve educational methods at prisons, jails, and juvenile facilities

Sec. 3041. Grant program to evaluate and improve educational methods at prisons, jails, and juvenile facilities

(a) Grant program authorized.—

The Attorney General may carry out a grant program under which the Attorney General may make grants to States, units of local government, territories, Indian Tribes, and other public and private entities to—

(1) evaluate methods to improve academic and vocational education for offenders in prisons, jails, and juvenile facilities;

(2) identify, and make recommendations to the Attorney General regarding, best practices relating to academic and vocational education for offenders in prisons, jails, and juvenile facilities, based on the evaluation under paragraph(1);

(3) improve the academic and vocational education programs (including technology career training) available to offenders in prisons, jails, and juvenile facilities; and

(4) implement methods to improve academic and vocational education for offenders in prisons, jails, and juvenile facilities consistent with the best practices identified in subsection (c).

(b) Application.—

To be eligible for a grant under this part, a State or other entity described in subsection (a) shall submit to the Attorney General an application in such form and manner, at such time, and accompanied by such information as the Attorney General specifies.

(c) Best practices.—

Not later than 180 days after the date of enactment of the Second Chance

Reauthorization Act of 2018, the Attorney General shall identify and publish best practices relating to academic and vocational education for offenders in prisons, jails, and juvenile facilities. The best practices shall consider the evaluations performed and recommendations made under grants made under subsection (a) before the date of enactment of the Second Chance Reauthorization Act of 2018.

(d) Report.—

Not later than 90 days after the last day of the final fiscal year of a grant under this part, each entity described in subsection (a) receiving such a grant shall submit to the Attorney General a detailed report of the

progress made by the entity using such grant, to permit the Attorney General to evaluate and improve academic and vocational education methods carried out with grants under this part; and

(3) in section 1001(a) of part J of title I of the Omnibus Crime Control and Safe Streets Act of 1968 (34 U.S.C. 10261(a) (https://www.law.cornell.edu/uscode/text/34/10261#a)), by adding at the end the following:

(28) There are authorized to be appropriated to carry out section 3031(a)(4) of part NN $5,000,000 for each of fiscal years 2019, 2020, 2021, 2022, and 2023.

(d) Careers training demonstration grants.—

Section 115 of the Second Chance Act of 2007 (34 U.S.C. 60511 (https://www.law.cornell.edu/uscode/text/34/60511)) is amended—

(1) in the heading, by striking "Technology careers" and inserting "Careers";

(2) in subsection (a)—

    (A) by striking "and Indian" and inserting "nonprofit organizations, and Indian"; and

    (B) by striking "technology career training to prisoners" and inserting "career training, including subsidized employment, when part of a training program, to prisoners and reentering youth and adults";

(3) in subsection (b)—

(A) by striking "technology careers training";

(B) by striking "technology-based";and

(C) by inserting ", as well as upon transition and reentry into the community" after "facility";

(4) by striking subsection(e);

(5) by redesignating subsections (c) and (d) as subsections (d) and (e), respectively;

(6) by inserting after subsection (b) the following:

(c) Priority consideration.—

Priority consideration shall be given to any application under this section that—

(1) provides assessment of local demand for employees in the geographic areas to which offenders are likely to return;

(2) conducts individualized reentry career planning upon the start of incarceration or post-release employment planning for each offender served under the grant;

(3) demonstrates connections to employers within the local community; or

(4) tracks and monitors employment outcomes; and

(7) by adding at the end the following:

(f) Authorization of appropriations.—

There are authorized to be appropriated to carry out this section $10,000,000 for each of fiscal years 2019, 2020, 2021, 2022, and 2023.

(e) Offender reentry substance abuse and criminal justice collaboration program.—

Section 201(f)(1) of the Second Chance Act of 2007 (34 U.S.C. 60521(f)(1) (https://www.law.cornell.edu/uscode/text/34/60521#f_1)) is amended to read as follows:

(1) In general.—

There are authorized to be appropriated to carry out this section $15,000,000

for each of fiscal years 2019 through 2023.

(f) Community-Based mentoring and transitional service grants to nonprofit
organizations.—

(1) In general.—

Section 211 of the Second Chance Act of 2007 (34 U.S.C.
60531 (https://www.law.cornell.edu/uscode/text/34/60531)) is
amended—

(A) in the header, by striking "Mentoring grants to nonprofit organizations" and
inserting "Community-based mentoring and transitional service grants to
nonprofit organizations";

(B) in subsection (a), by striking "mentoring and other";

(2) transitional services to assist in the reintegration of offenders into
the community, including—

(A) educational, literacy, and vocational, services and the
Transitional Jobs strategy;

(B) substance abuse treatment and services;

(C) coordinated supervision and services for offenders,
including physical health care and comprehensive housing
and mental health care;

(D) family services; and

(E) validated assessment tools to assess the risk factors of
returning inmates; and

(C) in subsection (b), by striking paragraph (2) and inserting the following:

(D) in subsection (f), by striking "this section" and all that follows and inserting the following: "this section $15,000,000 for each of fiscal years 2019 through 2023.".

(2) Table of contents amendment.—

The table of contents in section 2 of the Second Chance Act of 2007 (Public Law 110–199 (https://www.govtrack.us/search?q=PubLaw+110-199); 122 Stat. 657 (http://api.fdsys.gov/link?collection=statute&volume=122&page=657)) is amended by striking the item relating to section 211 and inserting the following:

Sec. 211. Community-based mentoring and transitional service grants.

(g) Definitions.—

(1) In general.—

Section 4 of the Second Chance Act of 2007 (34 U.S.C. 60502 (https://www.law.cornell.edu/uscode/text/34/60502)) is amended to read as follows:

Sec. 4. Definitions

In this Act—

(1) the term "exoneree" means an individual who—

(A) has been convicted of a Federal, tribal, or State offense that is punishable by a term of imprisonment of more than 1 year;

(B) has served a term of imprisonment for not less than 6 months in a Federal, tribal, or State prison or correctional facility as a result of the conviction described in subparagraph (A); and

(C) has been determined to be factually innocent of the offense described in subparagraph (A);

(2) the term "Indian tribe" has the meaning given in section 901 of title I of the Omnibus Crime Control and Safe Streets Act of 1968 (34 U.S.C. 10251 (https://www.law.cornell.edu/uscode/text/34/10251));

(3) the term "offender" includes an exoneree; and

(4) the term "Transitional Jobs strategy" means an employment strategy

for youth and adults who are chronically unemployed or those that have barriers to employment that—

(A) is conducted by State, tribal, and local governments, State, tribal, and local workforce boards, and nonprofit organizations;

(B) provides time-limited employment using individual placements, team placements, and social enterprise placements, without displacing existing employees;

(C) pays wages in accordance with applicable law, but in no event less than the higher of the rate specified in section 6(a)(1) of the Fair Labor Standards Act of 1938 (29 U.S.C. 206(a)(1) (https://www.law.cornell.edu/uscode/text/29/206#a_1)) or the applicable State or local minimum wage law, which are subsidized, in whole or in part, by public funds;

(D) combines time-limited employment with activities that promote skill development, remove barriers to employment, and lead to unsubsidized employment such as a thorough orientation and individual assessment, job readiness and life skills training, case management and supportive services, adult education and training, child support-related services, job retention support and incentives, and other similar activities;

(E) places participants into unsubsidized employment; and

(F) provides job retention, re-employment services, and continuing and vocational education to ensure continuing participation in unsubsidized employment and identification of opportunities for advancement.

(2) Table of contents amendment.—

The table of contents in section 2 of the Second Chance Act of 2007 (Public Law 110–199 (https://www.govtrack.us/search?q=PubLaw+110-199); 122 Stat. 657 (http://api.fdsys.gov/link?collection=statute&volume=122&page=657)) is amended by striking the item relating to section 4 and inserting the following:

Sec. 4. Definitions.

(h) Extension of the length of section 2976 grants.—

Section 6(1) of the Second Chance Act of 2007 (34 U.S.C. 60504(1) (https://www.law.cornell.edu/uscode/text/34/60504#1)) is amended by inserting "or under section 2976 of the Omnibus Crime Control and Safe Streets Act of 1968 (34 U.S.C. 10631 (https://www.law.cornell.edu/uscode/text/34/10631))" after "and 212".

Sec. 503. Audit and accountability of grantees

(a) Definitions.—

In this section—

(1) the term "covered grant program" means grants awarded under section 115, 201, or 211 of the Second Chance Act of 2007 (34 U.S.C. 60511 (https://www.law.cornell.edu/uscode/text/34/60511), 60521, and 60531), as amended by this title;

(2) the term "covered grantee" means a recipient of a grant from a covered grant program;

(3) the term "nonprofit", when used with respect to an organization, means an organization that is described in section 501(c)(3) of the Internal Revenue Code of 1986, and is exempt from taxation under section 501(a) of such Code; and

(4) the term "unresolved audit finding" means an audit report finding in a final audit report of the Inspector General of the Department of Justice that a covered grantee has used grant funds awarded to that grantee under a covered grant program for an unauthorized expenditure or otherwise unallowable cost that is not closed or resolved during a 12-month period prior to the date on which the final audit report is issued.

(b) Audit requirement.—

Beginning in fiscal year 2019, and annually thereafter, the Inspector General of the Department of Justice shall conduct audits of covered grantees to prevent waste, fraud, and abuse of funds awarded under covered grant programs. The Inspector General shall determine the appropriate number of covered grantees to be audited each year.

(c) Mandatory exclusion.—

A grantee that is found to have an unresolved audit finding under an audit conducted under subsection (b) may not receive grant funds under a covered grant program in the fiscal year following the fiscal year to which the finding relates.

(d) Reimbursement.—

If a covered grantee is awarded funds under the covered grant program from which it received a grant award during the 1-fiscal-year period during which the covered grantee is ineligible for an allocation of grant funds under subsection (c), the Attorney General shall—

(1) deposit into the General Fund of the Treasury an amount that is equal to the amount of the grant funds that were improperly awarded to the covered grantee; and

(2) seek to recoup the costs of the repayment to the Fund from the covered grantee that was improperly awarded the grant funds.

(e) Priority of grant awards.—

The Attorney General, in awarding grants under a covered grant program shall give priority to eligible entities that during the 2-year period preceding the application for a grant have not been found to have an unresolved audit finding.

(f) Nonprofit requirements.—

(1) Prohibition.—

A nonprofit organization that holds money in offshore accounts for the purpose of avoiding the tax described in section 511(a) of the Internal Revenue Code of 1986, shall not be eligible to receive, directly or indirectly, any funds from a covered grant program.

(2) Disclosure.—

Each nonprofit organization that is a covered grantee shall disclose in its application for such a grant, as a condition of receipt of such a grant, the compensation of its officers, directors, and trustees. Such disclosure shall include a description of the criteria relied on to determine such compensation.

(g) Prohibition on lobbying activity.—

(1) In general.—

Amounts made available under a covered grant program may not be used by any covered grantee to—

(A) lobby any representative of the Department of Justice regarding the award of grant funding; or

(B) lobby any representative of the Federal Government or a State, local, or tribal government regarding the award of grant funding.

(2) Penalty.—

If the Attorney General determines that a covered grantee has violated paragraph (1), the Attorney General shall—

(A) require the covered grantee to repay the grant in full; and

(B) prohibit the covered grantee from receiving a grant under the covered grant program from which it received a grant award during at least the 5-year period beginning on the date of such violation.

Sec. 504. Federal reentry improvements

(a) Responsible reintegration of offenders.—

Section 212 of the Second Chance Act of 2007 (34 U.S.C. 60532 (https://www.law.cornell.edu/uscode/text/34/60532)) is repealed.

(b) Federal prisoner reentry initiative.—

Section 231 of the Second Chance Act of 2007 (434 U.S.C. 60541 (https://www.law.cornell.edu/uscode/text/434/60541)) is amended—

(1) in subsection (g)—

(A) in paragraph (3), by striking "carried out during fiscal years 2009 and 2010" and inserting "carried out during fiscal years 2019 through 2023"; and

(B) in paragraph (5)(A)(ii), by striking "the greater of 10 years or";

(2) by striking subsection (h);

(3) by redesignating subsection (i) as subsection (h); and

(4) in subsection (h), as so redesignated, by striking "2009 and 2010" and inserting "2019 through 2023".

(c) Enhancing reporting requirements pertaining to community corrections.—

Section 3624(c) of title 18 (https://www.law.cornell.edu/uscode/text/18/3624#c), United States Code, is amended—

(1) in paragraph (5), in the second sentence, by inserting ", and number of prisoners not being placed in community corrections facilities for each reason set forth" before ", and any other information"; and

(2) in paragraph (6), by striking "the Second Chance Act of 2007" and inserting "the Second Chance Reauthorization Act of 2018".

(d) Termination of study on effectiveness of depot naltrexone for heroin addiction.—

Section 244 of the Second Chance Act of 2007 (34 U.S.C. 60554 (https://www.law.cornell.edu/uscode/text/34/60554)) is repealed.

(e) Authorization of appropriations for research.—

Section 245 of the Second Chance Act of 2007 (34 U.S.C. 60555 (https://www.law.cornell.edu/uscode/text/34/60555)) is amended—

(1) by striking "243, and 244" and inserting "and 243"; and

(2) by striking "$10,000,000 for each of the fiscal years 2009 and 2010" and inserting "$5,000,000 for each of the fiscal years 2019, 2020, 2021, 2022, and 2023".

(f) Federal prisoner recidivism reduction programming enhancement.—

(1) In general.—

Section 3621 of title 18 (https://www.law.cornell.edu/uscode/text/18/3621), United States Code, as amended by section 102(a) of this Act, is amended—

(A) by redesignating subsection (g) as subsection (i); and

(B) by inserting after subsection (f) the following:

The term "demonstrated to reduce recidivism" means that the

(g) **Partnerships To expand access to reentry programs proven To reduce recidivism.—**

(1) Definition.—

Director of Bureau of Prisons has determined that appropriate research has been conducted and has validated the effectiveness of the type of program on recidivism.

(2) Eligibility for recidivism reduction partnership.—

A faith-based or community-based nonprofit organization that provides mentoring or other programs that have been demonstrated to reduce recidivism is eligible to enter into a recidivism reduction partnership with a prison or community- based facility operated by the Bureau of Prisons.

(3) Recidivism reduction partnerships.—

The Director of the Bureau of Prisons shall develop policies to require wardens of prisons and community-based facilities to enter into recidivism reduction partnerships with faith-based and community-based nonprofit organizations that are willing to provide, on a volunteer basis, programs described in paragraph (2).

(4) Reporting requirement.—

The Director of the Bureau of Prisons shall submit to Congress an annual report on the last day of each fiscal year that—

(A) details, for each prison and community-based facility for the fiscal year just ended—

(i) the number of recidivism reduction partnerships under this section that were in effect;

(ii) the number of volunteers that provided recidivism reduction programming; and

(iii) the number of recidivism reduction programming hours

provided; and

  (B) explains any disparities between facilities in the numbers reported under subparagraph(A).

(2) Effective date.—

The amendments made by paragraph (1) shall take effect 180 days after the date of enactment of this Act.

(g) Repeals.—

(1) Section 2978 of title I of the Omnibus Crime Control and Safe Streets Act of 1968 (34 U.S.C. 10633 (https://www.law.cornell.edu/uscode/text/34/10633)) is repealed.

(2) Part CC of title I of the Omnibus Crime Control and Safe Streets Act of 1968 (34 U.S.C. 10581 (https://www.law.cornell.edu/uscode/text/34/10581) et seq.) is repealed.

Sec. 505. Federal interagency reentry coordination

(a) Reentry coordination.—

The Attorney General, in consultation with the Secretary of Housing and Urban Development, the Secretary of Labor, the Secretary of Education, the Secretary of Health and Human Services, the Secretary of Veterans Affairs, the Secretary of Agriculture, and the heads of such other agencies of the Federal Government as the Attorney General considers appropriate, and in collaboration with interested persons, service providers, nonprofit organizations, and State, tribal, and local governments, shall coordinate on Federal programs, policies, and activities relating to the reentry of individuals returning from incarceration to the community, with an emphasis on evidence-based practices and protection against duplication of services.

(b) Report.—

Not later than 2 years after the date of the enactment of this Act, the Attorney General, in consultation with the Secretaries listed in subsection (a), shall submit to Congress a report summarizing the achievements under subsection (a), and including recommendations for Congress that would further reduce barriers to successful reentry.

Sec. 506. Conference expenditures

(a) Limitation.—

No amounts authorized to be appropriated to the Department of Justice under this title, or any amendments made by this title, may be used by the Attorney General, or by any individual or organization awarded discretionary funds under this title, or any amendments made by this title, to host or support any expenditure for conferences that uses more than $20,000 in Department funds, unless the Deputy Attorney General or such Assistant Attorney Generals, Directors, or principal deputies as the Deputy Attorney General may designate, provides prior written authorization that the funds may be expended to host a conference. A conference that uses more than $20,000 in such funds, but less than an average of $500 in such funds for each attendee of the conference, shall not be subject to the limitations of this section.

(b) Written approval.—

Written approval under subsection (a) shall include a written estimate of all costs associated with the conference, including the cost of all food and beverages, audiovisual equipment, honoraria for speakers, and any entertainment.

(c) Report.—

The Deputy Attorney General shall submit an annual report to the Committee on the Judiciary of the Senate and the Committee on the Judiciary of the House of Representatives on all approved conference expenditures referenced in this section.

Sec. 507. Evaluation of the Second Chance Act program

(a) Evaluation of the second chance act grant program.—

Not later than 5 years after the date of enactment of this Act, the National Institute of Justice shall evaluate the effectiveness of grants used by the Department of Justice to support offender reentry and recidivism reduction programs at the State, local, Tribal, and Federal levels. The National Institute of Justice shall evaluate the following:

(1) The effectiveness of such programs in relation to their cost, including the extent to which the programs improve reentry outcomes, including employment, education, housing, reductions in recidivism, of participants in comparison to comparably situated individuals who did not participate in such programs and activities.

(2) The effectiveness of program structures and mechanisms for delivery of services.

(3) The impact of such programs on the communities and participants involved.

(4) The impact of such programs on related programs and activities.

(5) The extent to which such programs meet the needs of various demographic groups.

(6) The quality and effectiveness of technical assistance provided by the Department of Justice to grantees for implementing such programs.

(7) Such other factors as may be appropriate.

(b) Authorization of funds for evaluation.—

Not more than 1 percent of any amounts authorized to be appropriated to carry out the Second Chance Act grant program shall be made available to the National Institute of Justice each year to evaluate the processes, implementation, outcomes, costs, and effectiveness of the Second Chance Act grant program in improving reentry and reducing recidivism. Such funding may be used to provide support to grantees for supplemental data collection, analysis, and coordination associated with evaluation activities.

(c) Techniques.—

Evaluations conducted under this section shall use appropriate methodology and research designs. Impact evaluations conducted under this section shall include the use of intervention and control groups chosen by random assignment methods, to the extent possible.

(d) Metrics and Outcomes for Evaluation.—

(1) In general.—

Not later than 180 days after the date of enactment of this Act, the National Institute of Justice shall consult with relevant stakeholders and identify outcome measures, including employment, housing, education, and public safety, that are to be achieved by programs authorized under the Second Chance Act grant program and the metrics by which the achievement of such outcomes shall be determined.

(2) Publication.—

Not later than 30 days after the date on which the National Institute of Justice identifies metrics and outcomes under paragraph (1), the Attorney General shall publish such metrics and outcomes identified.

(e) Data collection.—

As a condition of award under the Second Chance Act grant program (including a subaward under section 3021(b) of title I of the Omnibus Crime Control and Safe Streets Act of 1968 (34 U.S.C. 10701(b) (https://www.law.cornell.edu/uscode/text/34/10701#b))), grantees shall be required to collect and report to the Department of Justice data based upon the metrics identified under subsection (d). In accordance with applicable law, collection of individual-level data under a pledge of confidentiality shall be protected by the National Institute of Justice in accordance with such pledge.

(f) Data accessibility.—

Not later than 5 years after the date of enactment of this Act, the National Institute of Justice shall—

(1) make data collected during the course of evaluation under this section available in de-identified form in such a manner that reasonably protects a pledge of confidentiality to participants under subsection (e); and

(2) make identifiable data collected during the course of evaluation under this section available to qualified researchers for future research and evaluation, in accordance with applicable law.

(g) Publication and reporting of evaluation findings.—

The National Institute of Justice shall—

(1) not later than 365 days after the date on which the enrollment of participants in an impact evaluation is completed, publish an interim report on such evaluation;

(2) not later than 90 days after the date on which any evaluation is completed, publish and make publicly available such evaluation; and

(3) not later than 60 days after the completion date described in paragraph (2), submit a report to the Committee on the Judiciary of the House of Representatives and the Committee on the Judiciary of the Senate on such evaluation.

(h) Second Chance Act grant program defined.—

In this section, the term "Second Chance Act grant program" means any grant program reauthorized under this title and the amendments made by this title.

Sec. 508. GAO review

Not later than 3 years after the date of enactment of the First Step Act of 2018 the Comptroller General of the United States shall conduct a review of all of the grant awards made under this title and amendments made by this title that includes—

(1) an evaluation of the effectiveness of the reentry programs funded by grant awards under this title and amendments made by this title at reducing recidivism, including a determination of which reentry programs were most effective;

(2) recommendations on how to improve the effectiveness of reentry programs, including those for which prisoners may earn time credits under the First Step Act of 2018; and

(3) an evaluation of the effectiveness of mental health services, drug treatment, medical care, job training and placement, educational services, and vocational services programs funded under this title and amendments made by this title.

Title VI

Miscellaneous criminal justice

Sec. 601. Placement of prisoners close to families

Section 3621(b) of title 18 (https://www.law.cornell.edu/uscode/text/18/3621#b), United States Code, is amended—

(1) by striking "shall designate the place of the prisoner's imprisonment." and inserting "shall designate the place of the prisoner's imprisonment, and shall, subject to bed availability, the prisoner's security designation, the prisoner's programmatic needs, the prisoner's mental and medical health needs, any request made by the prisoner related to faith-based needs, recommendations of the sentencing court, and other security concerns of the Bureau of Prisons, place the prisoner in a facility as close as practicable to the prisoner's primary residence, and to the extent practicable, in a facility within 500 driving miles of that residence. The Bureau shall, subject to consideration of the factors described in the preceding sentence and the prisoner's preference for staying at his or her current facility or being transferred, transfer prisoners to facilities that are closer to the prisoner's primary residence even if the prisoner is already in a facility within 500 driving miles of that residence."; and

(2) by adding at the end the following: "Notwithstanding any other provision of law, a designation of a place of imprisonment under this subsection is not reviewable by

any court.".

Sec. 602. Home confinement for low-risk prisoners

Section 3624(c)(2) of title 18 (https://www.law.cornell.edu/uscode/text/18/3624#c_2), United States Code, is amended by adding at the end the following: "The Bureau of Prisons shall, to the extent practicable, place prisoners with lower risk levels and lower needs on home confinement for the maximum amount of time permitted under this paragraph.".

Sec. 603. Federal prisoner reentry initiative reauthorization; modification of imposed term of imprisonment

(a) Federal prisoner reentry initiative reauthorization.—

Section 231(g) of the Second Chance Act of 2007 (34 U.S.C. 60541(g)

(1) in paragraph (1)—

    (A) by inserting "and eligible terminally ill offenders" after "elderly offenders" each place the term appears;

    (B) in subparagraph (A), by striking "a Bureau of Prisons facility" and inserting "Bureau of Prisons facilities";

    (C) in subparagraph (B)—

        (i) by striking "the Bureau of Prisons facility" and inserting "Bureau of Prisons facilities"; and

        (ii) by inserting ", upon written request from either the Bureau of Prisons or an eligible elderly offender or eligible terminally ill offender" after "to home detention"; and

    (D) in subparagraph (C), by striking "the Bureau of Prisons facility" and inserting "Bureau of Prisons facilities";

(2) in paragraph (2), by inserting "or eligible terminally ill offender" after "elderly offender";

(3) in paragraph (3), as amended by section 504(b)(1)(A) of this Act, by striking "at least one Bureau of Prisons facility" and inserting "Bureau of Prisons facilities"; and

(4) in paragraph (4)—

    (A) by inserting "or eligible terminally ill offender" after "each eligible elderly offender"; and

    (B) by inserting "and eligible terminally ill offenders" after "eligible elderly offenders"; and

(5) in paragraph (5)—

    (A) in subparagraph (A)—

        (i) in clause (i), striking "65 years of age" and inserting "60 years of age"; and

(ii) in clause (ii), as amended by section 504(b)(1)(B) of this Act, by striking "75 percent" and inserting "2/3"; and

(B) by adding at the end the following:

(D) Eligible terminally illoffender.—

The term "eligible terminally ill offender" means an offender in the custody of the Bureau of Prisons who—

(i) is serving a term of imprisonment based on conviction for an offense or offenses that do not include any crime of violence (as defined in section 16(a) of title 18 (https://www.law.cornell.edu/uscode/text/18/16#a), United States Code), sex offense (as defined in section 111(5) of the Sex Offender Registration and Notification Act (34 U.S.C. 20911(5) (https://www.law.cornell.edu/uscode/text/34/20911#5))), offense described in section 2332b(g)(5)(B) of title 18 (https://www.law.cornell.edu/uscode/text/18/2332b#g_5_B), United States Code, or offense under chapter 37 of title 18, United States Code;

(ii) satisfies the criteria specified in clauses (iii) through (vii) of subparagraph (A); and

(iii) has been determined by a medical doctor approved by the Bureau of Prisons to be—

(I) in need of care at a nursing home, intermediate care facility, or assisted living facility, as those terms are defined in section 232 of the National Housing Act (12 U.S.C. 1715w (https://www.law.cornell.edu/uscode/text/12/1715w)); or

(II) diagnosed with a terminal illness.

(b) Increasing the use and transparency of compassionate release.—

Section 3582 of title 18 (https://www.law.cornell.edu/uscode/text/18/3582), United States Code, is amended—

(1) in subsection (c)(1)(A), in the matter preceding clause (i), by inserting after "Bureau of Prisons," the following: "or upon motion of the defendant after the defendant has fully exhausted all administrative rights to appeal a failure of the Bureau of Prisons to bring a motion on the defendant's behalf or the lapse of 30 days from the receipt of such a request by the warden of the defendant's facility, whichever is earlier,";

(2) by redesignating subsection (d) as subsection (e); and

(3) by inserting after subsection (c) the following:

> (d) Notification requirements.—
>
> > (1) Terminal illness defined.—
> >
> > In this subsection, the term "terminal illness" means a disease or condition with an end-of-life trajectory.
> >
> > (2) Notification.—
> >
> > The Bureau of Prisons shall, subject to any applicable confidentiality requirements—
> >
> > (A) in the case of a defendant diagnosed with a terminal illness—
> >
> > > (i) not later than 72 hours after the diagnosis notify the defendant's attorney, partner, and family members of the defendant's condition and inform the defendant's attorney, partner, and family members that they may prepare and submit on the defendant's behalf a request for a sentence reduction pursuant to subsection(c)(1)(A);
> > >
> > > (ii) not later than 7 days after the date of the diagnosis, provide the defendant's partner and family members (including extended family) with an opportunity to visit the defendant in person;
> > >
> > > (iii) upon request from the defendant or his attorney, partner, or a family member, ensure that Bureau of Prisons employees assist the defendant in the preparation, drafting, and submission of a request for a sentence reduction pursuant to

subsection (c)(1) (A); and

    (iv) not later than 14 days of receipt of a request for a sentence reduction submitted on the defendant's behalf by the defendant or the defendant's attorney, partner, or family member, process the request;

(B) in the case of a defendant who is physically or mentally unable to submit a request for a sentence reduction pursuant to subsection (c)(1)(A)—

    (i) inform the defendant's attorney, partner, and family members that they may prepare and submit on the defendant's behalf a request for a sentence reduction pursuant to subsection (c)(1) (A);

    (ii) accept and process a request for sentence reduction that has been prepared and submitted on the defendant's behalf by the defendant's attorney, partner, or family member under clause (i); and

    (iii) upon request from the defendant or his attorney, partner, or family member, ensure that Bureau of Prisons employees assist the defendant in the preparation, drafting, and submission of a request for a sentence reduction pursuant to subsection (c)(1) (A); and

(C) ensure that all Bureau of Prisons facilities regularly and visibly post, including in prisoner handbooks, staff training materials, and facility law libraries and medical and hospice facilities, and make available to prisoners upon demand, notice of—

    (i) a defendant's ability to request a sentence reduction pursuant to subsection (c)(1)(A);

    (ii) the procedures and timelines for initiating and resolving requests described in clause (i); and

    (iii) the right to appeal a denial of a request described in clause (i) after all administrative rights to appeal within the Bureau of Prisons have been exhausted.

(3) Annual report.—

Not later than 1 year after the date of enactment of this subsection, and once every year thereafter, the Director of the Bureau of Prisons shall submit to the Committee on the Judiciary of the Senate and the Committee on the Judiciary of the House of Representatives a report on requests for sentence reductions pursuant to subsection (c)(1)(A), which shall include a description of, for the previous year—

(A) the number of prisoners granted and denied sentence reductions, categorized by the criteria relied on as the grounds for a reduction in sentence;

(B) the number of requests initiated by or on behalf of prisoners, categorized by the criteria relied on as the grounds for a reduction in sentence;

(C) the number of requests that Bureau of Prisons employees assisted prisoners in drafting, preparing, or submitting, categorized by the criteria relied on as the grounds for a reduction in sentence, and the final decision made in each request;

(D) the number of requests that attorneys, partners, or family members submitted on a defendant's behalf, categorized by the criteria relied on as the grounds for a reduction in sentence, and the final decision made in each request;

(E) the number of requests approved by the Director of the Bureau of Prisons, categorized by the criteria relied on as the grounds for a reduction in sentence;

(F) the number of requests denied by the Director of the Bureau of Prisons and the reasons given for each denial, categorized by the criteria relied on as the grounds for a reduction in sentence;

(G) for each request, the time elapsed between the date the request was received by the warden and the final decision, categorized by the criteria relied on as the grounds for a reduction in sentence;

(H) for each request, the number of prisoners who died while their request was pending and, for each, the amount of time that had elapsed between the date the request was received by the Bureau of Prisons, categorized by the criteria relied on as the grounds for a reduction in sentence;

(I) the number of Bureau of Prisons notifications to attorneys, partners, and family members of their right to visit a terminally ill defendant as required under paragraph (2)(A)(ii) and, for each, whether a visit occurred and how much time elapsed between the notification and the visit;

(J) the number of visits to terminally ill prisoners that were denied by the Bureau of Prisons due to security or other concerns, and the reasons given for each denial; and

(K) the number of motions filed by defendants with the court after all administrative rights to appeal a denial of a sentence reduction had been exhausted, the outcome of each motion, and the time that had elapsed between the date the request was first received by the Bureau of Prisons and the date the defendant filed the motion with the court.

Sec. 604. Identification for returning citizens

(a) Identification and release assistance for Federal prisoners.—

Section 231(b) of the Second Chance Act of 2007 (34 U.S.C. 60541(b) (https://www.law.cornell.edu/uscode/text/34/60541#b)) is amended—

(1) in paragraph (1)—

(A) by striking "(including" and inserting "prior to release from a term of imprisonment in a Federal prison or if the individual was not sentenced to a term of imprisonment in a Federal prison, prior to release from a sentence to a term in community confinement, including"; and

(B) by striking "or birth certificate) prior to release" and inserting "and a birth certificate"; and

(2) by adding at the end the following:

(4) Definition.—

In this subsection, the term "community confinement" means residence in a community treatment **center**, halfway house, restitution center, mental health facility, alcohol or drug rehabilitation center, or other community facility.

(b) Duties of the Bureau of Prisons.—

Section 4042(a) of title 18 (https://www.law.cornell.edu/uscode/text/18/4042#a), United States Code, is amended—

(1) by redesignating paragraphs (D) and (E) as paragraphs (6) and (7), respectively;

(2) in paragraph (6) (as so redesignated)—

    (A) in clause (i)—

        (i) by striking "Social Security Cards,"; and

        (ii) by striking "and" at the end;

    (B) by redesignating clause (ii) as clause (iii);

    (C) by inserting after clause (i) the following:

        (ii) obtain identification, including a social security card, driver's license or other official photo identification, and a birth certificate; and

    (D) in clause (iii) (as so redesignated), by inserting after "prior to release" the following: "from a sentence to a term of imprisonment in a Federal prison or if the individual was not sentenced to a term of imprisonment in a Federal prison, prior to release from a sentence to a term of community confinement"; and

    (E) by redesignating clauses (i), (ii), and (iii) (as so amended) as subparagraphs (A), (B), and (C), respectively, and adjusting the margins accordingly; and

116

(3) in paragraph (7) (as so redesignated), by redesignating clauses (i) through (vii) as subparagraphs (A) through (G), respectively, and adjusting the margins accordingly.

Sec. 605. Expanding inmate employment through Federal Prison Industries

(a) New market authorizations.—

Chapter 307 of title 18, United States Code, is amended by inserting after section 4129 the following:

Sec. 4130. Additional markets

(a) In general.—

Except as provided in subsection (b), notwithstanding any other provision of law, Federal Prison Industries may sell products to—

(1) public entities for use in penal or correctional institutions;

(2) public entities for use in disaster relief or emergency response;

(3) the government of the District of Columbia; and

(4) any organization described in subsection (c)(3), (c)(4), or (d) of section 501 of the Internal Revenue Code of 1986 that is exempt from taxation under section 501(a) of such Code.

(b) Office furniture.—

Federal Prison Industries may not sell office furniture to the organizations described in subsection (a)(4).

(c) Definitions.—

In this section:

(1) The term "office furniture" means any product or service offering intended to meet the furnishing needs of the workplace, including office, healthcare, educational, and hospitality environments.

(2) The term "public entity" means a State, a subdivision of a State, an Indian tribe, and an agency or governmental corporation or business of any of

the foregoing.

    (3) The term "State" means a State, the District of Columbia, the Commonwealth of Puerto Rico, Guam, American Samoa, the Northern Mariana Islands, and the United States Virgin Islands.

(b) Technical amendment.—

The table of sections for chapter 307 of title 18, United States Code, is amended by inserting after the item relating to section 4129 the following:

    4130. Additional markets.

(c) Deferred compensation.—

Section 4126(c)(4) of title 18 (https://www.law.cornell.edu/uscode/text/18/4126#c_4), United States Code, is amended by inserting after "operations," the following: "not less than 15 percent of such compensation for any inmate shall be reserved in the fund or a separate account and made available to assist the inmate with costs associated with release from prison,".

(d) GAO report.—

Beginning not later than 90 days after the date of enactment of this Act, the Comptroller General of the United States shall conduct an audit of Federal Prison Industries that includes the following:

(1) An evaluation of Federal Prison Industries's effectiveness in reducing recidivism compared to other rehabilitative programs in the prison system.

(2) An evaluation of the scope and size of the additional markets made available to Federal Prison Industries under this section and the total market value that would be opened up to Federal Prison Industries for competition with private sector providers of products and services.

(3) An evaluation of whether the following factors create an unfair competitive environment between Federal Prison Industries and private sector providers of products and services which would be exacerbated by further expansion:

    (A) Federal Prison Industries's status as a mandatory source of supply for Federal agencies and the requirement that the buying agency must obtain a waiver in order to make a competitive purchase from the private sector if the item to be acquired is listed on the schedule of products and services published by Federal Prison Industries.

(B) Federal Prison Industries's ability to determine that the price to be paid by Federal Agencies is fair and reasonable, rather than such a determination being made by the buying agency.

(C) An examination of the extent to which Federal Prison Industries is bound by the requirements of the generally applicable Federal Acquisition Regulation pertaining to the conformity of the delivered product with the specified design and performance specifications and adherence to the delivery schedule required by the Federal agency, based on the transactions being categorized as interagency transfers.

(D) An examination of the extent to which Federal Prison Industries avoids transactions that are little more than pass through transactions where the work provided by inmates does not create meaningful value or meaningful work opportunities for inmates.

(E) The extent to which Federal Prison Industries must comply with the same worker protection, workplace safety and similar regulations applicable to, and enforceable against, Federal contractors.

(F) The wages Federal Prison Industries pays to inmates, taking into account inmate productivity and other factors such as security concerns associated with having a facility in a prison.

(G) The effect of any additional cost advantages Federal Prison Industries has over private sector providers of goods and services, including—

   (i) the costs absorbed by the Bureau of Prisons such as inmate medical care and infrastructure expenses including real estate and utilities; and

   (ii) its exemption from Federal and State income taxes and property taxes.

(4) An evaluation of the extent to which the customers of Federal Prison Industries are satisfied with quality, price, and timely delivery of the products and services provided it provides, including summaries of other independent assessments such as reports of agency inspectors general, if applicable.

Sec. 606. De-escalation training

Beginning not later than 1 year after the date of enactment of this Act, the Director of the Bureau of Prisons shall incorporate into training programs provided to officers and employees of the Bureau of Prisons (including officers and employees of an organization with which the Bureau of Prisons has a contract to provide services relating to imprisonment) specialized and comprehensive training in procedures to—

(1) de-escalate encounters between a law enforcement officer or an officer or employee of the Bureau of Prisons, and a civilian or a prisoner (as such term is defined in section 3635 of title 18 (https://www.law.cornell.edu/uscode/text/18/3635), United States Code, as added by section 101(a) of this Act); and

(2) identify and appropriately respond to incidents that involve the unique needs of individuals who have a mental illness or cognitive deficit.

Sec. 607. Evidence-Based treatment for opioid and heroin abuse

(a) Report on evidence-based treatment for opioid and heroin abuse.—

Not later than 90 days after the date of enactment of this Act, the Director of the Bureau of Prisons shall submit to the Committees on the Judiciary and the Committees on Appropriations of the Senate and of the House of Representatives a report assessing the availability of and the capacity of the Bureau of Prisons to treat heroin and opioid abuse through evidence-based programs, including medication-assisted treatment where appropriate. In preparing the report, the Director shall consider medication-assisted treatment as a strategy to assist in treatment where appropriate and not as a replacement for holistic and other drug-free approaches. The report shall include a description of plans to expand access to evidence-based treatment for heroin and opioid abuse for prisoners, including access to medication-assisted treatment in appropriate cases. Following submission, the Director shall take steps to implement these plans.

(b) Report on the availability of medication-Assisted treatment for opioid and heroin abuse, and implementation thereof.—

Not later than 120 days after the date of enactment of this Act, the Director of the Administrative Office of the United States Courts shall submit to the Committees on the Judiciary and the Committees on Appropriations of the Senate and of the House of Representatives a report assessing the availability of and capacity for the provision of medication-assisted treatment for opioid and heroin abuse by treatment service providers serving prisoners who are serving a term of supervised release, and including a description of plans to expand access to medication-assisted treatment for heroin and opioid abuse whenever appropriate among prisoners under supervised release. Following submission, the Director will take steps to implement these plans.

Sec. 608. Pilot programs

(a) In general.—

The Bureau of Prisons shall establish each of the following pilot programs for 5 years, in at least 20 facilities:

(1) Mentorship for youth.—

A program to pair youth with volunteers from faith-based or community organizations, which may include formerly incarcerated offenders, that have relevant experience or expertise in mentoring, and a willingness to serve as a mentor in such a capacity.

(2) Service to abandoned, rescued, or otherwise vulnerable animals.—

A program to equip prisoners with the skills to provide training and therapy to animals seized by Federal law enforcement under asset forfeiture authority and to organizations that provide shelter and similar services to abandoned, rescued, or otherwise vulnerable animals.

(b) Reporting requirement.—

Not later than 1 year after the conclusion of the pilot programs, the Attorney General shall report to Congress on the results of the pilot programs under this section. Such report shall include cost savings, numbers of participants, and information about recidivism rates among participants.

(c) Definition.—

In this title, the term "youth" means a prisoner (as such term is defined in section 3635 of title 18 (https://www.law.cornell.edu/uscode/text/18/3635), United States Code, as added by section 101(a) of this Act) who was 21 years of age or younger at the time of the commission or alleged commission of the criminal offense for which the individual is being prosecuted or serving a term of imprisonment, as the case may be.

Sec. 609. Ensuring supervision of released sexually dangerous persons

(a) Probation officers.—

Section 3603 of title 18 (https://www.law.cornell.edu/uscode/text/18/3603), United

States Code, is amended in paragraph (8)(A) by striking "or 4246" and inserting ", 4246, or 4248".

(b) Pretrial services officers.—

Section 3154 of title 18 (https://www.law.cornell.edu/uscode/text/18/3154), United States Code, is amended in paragraph (12)(A) by striking "or 4246" and inserting ", 4246, or 4248".

Sec. 610. Data collection

(a) National Prisoner Statistics Program.—

Beginning not later than 1 year after the date of enactment of this Act, and annually thereafter, pursuant to the authority under section 302 of the Omnibus Crime Control and Safe Streets Act of 1968 (42 U.S.C. 3732 (https://www.law.cornell.edu/uscode/text/42/3732)), the Director of the Bureau of Justice Statistics, with information that shall be provided by the Director of the Bureau of Prisons, shall include in the National Prisoner Statistics Program the following:

(1) The number of prisoners (as such term is defined in section 3635 of title 18 (https://www.law.cornell.edu/uscode/text/18/3635), United States Code, as added by section 101(a) of this Act) who are veterans of the Armed Forces of the United States.

(2) The number of prisoners who have been placed in solitary confinement at any time during the previous year.

(3) The number of female prisoners known by the Bureau of Prisons to be pregnant, as well as the outcomes of such pregnancies, including information on pregnancies that result in live birth, stillbirth, miscarriage, abortion, ectopic pregnancy, maternal death, neonatal death, and preterm birth.

(4) The number of prisoners who volunteered to participate in a substance abuse treatment program, and the number of prisoners who have participated in such a program.

(5) The number of prisoners provided medication-assisted treatment with medication approved by the Food and Drug Administration while in custody in order to treat substance use disorder.

(6) The number of prisoners who were receiving medication-assisted treatment with medication approved by the Food and Drug Administration prior to the

commencement of their term of imprisonment.

(7) The number of prisoners who are the parent or guardian of a minor child.

(8) The number of prisoners who are single, married, or otherwise in a committed relationship.

(9) The number of prisoners who have not achieved a GED, high school diploma, or equivalent prior to entering prison.

(10) The number of prisoners who, during the previous year, received their GED or other equivalent certificate while incarcerated.

(11) The numbers of prisoners for whom English is a second language.

(12) The number of incidents, during the previous year, in which restraints were used on a female prisoner during pregnancy, labor, or postpartum recovery, as well as information relating to the type of restraints used, and the circumstances under which each incident occurred.

(13) The vacancy rate for medical and healthcare staff positions, and average length of such a vacancy.

(14) The number of facilities that operated, at any time during the previous year, without at least 1 clinical nurse, certified paramedic, or licensed physician on site.

(15) The number of facilities that during the previous year were accredited by the American Correctional Association.

(16) The number and type of recidivism reduction partnerships described in section 3621(h)(5) of title 18 (https://www.law.cornell.edu/uscode/text/18/3621#h_5), United States Code, as added by section 102(a) of this Act, entered into by each facility.

(17) The number of facilities with remote learning capabilities.

(18) The number of facilities that offer prisoners video conferencing.

(19) Any changes in costs related to legal phone calls and visits following implementation of section 3632(d)(1) of title 18 (https://www.law.cornell.edu/uscode/text/18/3632#d_1), United States Code, as

added by section 101(a) of this Act.

(20) The number of aliens in prison during the previous year.

(21) For each Bureau of Prisons facility, the total number of violations that resulted in reductions in rewards, incentives, or time credits, the number of such violations for each category of violation, and the demographic breakdown of the prisoners who have received such reductions.

(22) The number of assaults on Bureau of Prisons staff by prisoners and the number of criminal prosecutions of prisoners for assaulting Bureau of Prisons staff.

(23) The capacity of each recidivism reduction program and productive activity to accommodate eligible inmates at each Bureau of Prisons facility.

(24) The number of volunteers who were certified to volunteer in a Bureau of Prisons facility, broken down by level (level I and level II), and by each Bureau of Prisons facility.

(25) The number of prisoners enrolled in recidivism reduction programs and productive activities at each Bureau of Prisons facility, broken down by risk level and by program, and the number of those enrolled prisoners who successfully completed each program.

(26) The breakdown of prisoners classified at each risk level by demographic characteristics, including age, sex, race, and the length of the sentence imposed.

(b) Report to Judiciary committees.—

Beginning not later than 1 year after the date of enactment of this Act, and annually thereafter for a period of 7 years, the Director of the Bureau of Justice Statistics shall submit a report containing the information described in paragraphs (1) through (26) of subsection (a) to the Committee on the Judiciary of the Senate and the Committee on the Judiciary of the House of Representatives.

Sec. 611. Healthcare products

(a) Availability.—

The Director of the Bureau of Prisons shall make the healthcare products described in subsection (c) available to prisoners for free, in a quantity that is appropriate to the healthcare needs of each prisoner.

(b) Quality products.—

The Director shall ensure that the healthcare products provided under this section conform with applicable industry standards.

(c) Products.—

The healthcare products described in this subsection are tampons and sanitary napkins.

Sec. 612. Adult and juvenile collaboration programs

Section 2991 of title I of the Omnibus Crime Control and Safe Streets Act of 1968 (34 U.S.C. 10651 (https://www.law.cornell.edu/uscode/text/34/10651)) is amended—

(1) in subsection (b)(4)—

  (A) by striking subparagraph (D); and

  (B) by redesignating subparagraph (E) as subparagraph (D);

(2) in subsection (e), by striking "may use up to 3 percent" and inserting "shall use not less than 6 percent"; and

(3) by amending subsection (g) to read as follows:

  (g) Collaboration set-aside.—

  The Attorney General shall use not less than 8 percent of funds appropriated to provide technical assistance to State and local governments receiving grants under this part to foster collaboration between such governments in furtherance of the purposes set forth in section 3 of the Mentally Ill Offender Treatment and Crime Reduction Act of 2004 (34 U.S.C. 10651 (https://www.law.cornell.edu/uscode/text/34/10651) note).

Sec. 613. Juvenile solitary confinement

(a) In general.—

Chapter 403 of title 18, United States Code, is amended by adding at the end the following:

Sec. 5043. Juvenile solitary confinement

(a) Definitions.—

In this section—

(1) the term "covered juvenile" means—

(A) a juvenile who—

(i) is being proceeded against under this chapter for an alleged act of juvenile delinquency; or
(ii) has been adjudicated delinquent under this chapter; or

(B) a juvenile who is being proceeded against as an adult in a district court of the United States for an alleged criminal offense;

(2) the term "juvenile facility" means any facility where covered juveniles are—

(A) committed pursuant to an adjudication of delinquency under this chapter; or

(B) detained prior to disposition or conviction; and

(3) the term "room confinement" means the involuntary placement of a covered juvenile alone in a cell, room, or other area for any reason.

(b) Prohibition on room confinement in juvenile facilities.—

(1) In general.—

The use of room confinement at a juvenile facility for discipline, punishment, retaliation, or any reason other than as a temporary response to a covered juvenile's behavior that poses a serious and immediate risk of physical harm to any individual, including the covered juvenile, is prohibited.

(2) Juveniles posing risk of harm.—

(A) Requirement to use least restrictive techniques.—

(i) In general.—

Before a staff member of a juvenile facility places a covered juvenile in room confinement, the staff member shall attempt to use less restrictive techniques, including—

(I) talking with the covered juvenile in an attempt to de-escalate the situation; and

(II) permitting a qualified mental health professional to talk to the covered juvenile.

(ii) Explanation.—

If, after attempting to use less restrictive techniques as required under clause (i), a staff member of a juvenile facility decides to place a covered juvenile in room confinement, the staff member shall first—

(I) explain to the covered juvenile the reasons for the room confinement; and

(II) inform the covered juvenile that release from room confinement will occur—
(aa) immediately when the covered juvenile regains self-control, as described in subparagraph (B)(i); or
(bb) not later than after the expiration of the time period described in subclause (I) or (II) of subparagraph (B)(ii), as applicable.

(B) Maximum period of confinement.—

If a covered juvenile is placed in room confinement because the covered juvenile poses a serious and immediate risk of physical harm to himself or herself, or to others, the covered juvenile shall be released—

(i) immediately when the covered juvenile has sufficiently gained control so as to no longer engage in behavior that threatens serious and immediate risk of physical harm to himself or herself, or to others; or

(ii) if a covered juvenile does not sufficiently gain control as described in clause (i), not later than—

(I) 3 hours after being placed in room confinement, in the case of a covered juvenile who poses a serious and immediate risk of physical harm to others; or

(II) 30 minutes after being placed in room confinement, in the case of a covered juvenile who poses a serious and immediate risk of physical harm only to himself or herself.

(C) Risk of harm after maximum period of confinement.—

If, after the applicable maximum period of confinement under subclause (I) or (II) of subparagraph (B)(ii) has expired, a covered juvenile continues to pose a serious and immediate risk of physical harm described in that subclause—

(i) the covered juvenile shall be transferred to another juvenile facility or internal location where services can be provided to the covered juvenile without relying on room confinement; or

(ii) if a qualified mental health professional believes the level of crisis service needed is not currently available, a staff member of the juvenile facility shall initiate a referral to a location that can meet the needs of the covered juvenile.

(D) Spirit and purpose.—

The use of consecutive periods of room confinement to evade the spirit and purpose of this subsection shall be prohibited.

(b) Technical and conforming amendment.—

The table of sections for chapter 403 of title 18, United States Code, is amended by adding at the end the following:

5043. Juvenile solitary confinement.

Made in the USA
Columbia, SC
09 January 2022

53869114R00081